"Searing, lucid, tender, and wise, *The Year of the Horses* is a moving, beautifully written interrogation into a complicated, privileged childhood and its aftermath. Courtney Maum weaves together the sensory, tactile world of horses and their capacity to heal us, along with one of the most illuminating and powerful depictions of depression I have ever read. Oh, and it's also a page-turner. I tore through it with immense pleasure."

—**DANI SHAPIRO**, bestselling author of *Inheritance: A Memoir of Genealogy, Paternity, and Love*

"Gorgeously written, wry but loving, heartbreaking and, most of all, roving . . . *The Year of the Horses* is a memoir of power and beauty and pain that moves across the world like the beautiful horses that carry it."

—**LISA TADDEO**, bestselling author of *Animal*

"Tender, honest, and beautifully written."

—**KATE BAER**, bestselling author of *What Kind of Woman*

"If, like me at age fifty, you have a hankering to resume riding again (never mind that it's been thirty-four years), this is the book for you. Courtney will show you her way to this particular form of personal salvation."

—**SALLY MANN**, National Book Award finalist and author of *Hold Still: A Memoir with Photographs*

"Courtney Maum dives into her own life with the same fearlessness and honesty that she brings to her fiction. *The Year of the Horses* is a beautiful, unflinching exploration of darkness and self-forgiveness, terror and tenderness."

—**HALA ALYAN**, author of *The Arsonists' City*

"Here is a book where the author writes not from an ideal of who she should be, but as she is. It lacks performative overtones or those typical bits where the reader is assured the author is self-aware. No, it's nothing like that. *The Year of the Horses* sings like the world actually feels, it gives us permission to be who we are, and it's written by one of the best—a writer's writer—with a maturity that reveals her decades-long devotion to her craft."

—**HOLLY WHITAKER**, bestselling author of *Quit Like a Woman: The Radical Choice to Not Drink in a Culture Obsessed with Alcohol*

"The concept of finding safety in a dangerous sport won't make sense to everyone, but the way that Courtney found meaning and magic in horses resonates with me. As a polo player, I loved the sometimes laugh-out-loud journey of an adult trying against all odds to learn the sport of kings. This is a great memoir that somehow manages to be both deeply moving and funny."

—**KAREEM ROSSER**, author of *Crossing the Line: A Fearless Team of Brothers and the Sport That Changed Their Lives Forever*

THE YEAR OF THE HORSES

Published by Tin House, Portland, Oregon

Distributed by W. W. Norton & Company

Library of Congress Cataloging-in-Publication Data is available

First US Edition 2022
Printed in the USA
Interior design by Diane Chonette

www.tinhouse.com

THE YEAR OF THE HORSES

A MEMOIR

COURTNEY MAUM

TIN HOUSE / Portland, Oregon

ALSO BY COURTNEY MAUM

I Am Having So Much Fun Here Without You

Touch

Costalegre

Before and After the Book Deal: A Writer's Guide to Finishing, Publishing, Promoting and Surviving Your First Book

For my firefighters

For now just remember how you felt the day you were born: desperate for magic, ready to love.

—KATE BAER, *What Kind of Woman*

AUTHOR'S NOTE

To write this book, I returned to my child's mind and embraced its bias, its subjectivity, and its tenderness. Allowing for the indulgences of my adult memory, this is a work of nonfiction, except for a handful of names and identifying details I have changed to respect individuals' privacy.

1

THE NIGHT MARE

I am standing by our front door as my daughter works her socks on. She is two years old, her blond wisps curling from exertion. The socks are pink or they are white—it doesn't matter, because they are not socks, they are the enemy.

"Just put your socks on, honey," I say, willing mercy from the lava building up inside me. "Just pull them on."

My daughter scrunches her face into a protest of discomfort. The toe seams have to be perfectly aligned across the tip-top of each toe. The heel pads have to fit neatly over the heels. The big-girl tugging on of my toddler's socks can take upwards of eight minutes. Every. Single. Morning.

My husband, Leo, is out scouting a location for a film he is trying to raise money for. Or he is outside on the phone begging for that money in the one spot on our dirt road where we get two bars. I have lost track of his end goal, I've lost track of where he is; it seems to me that every day is a déjà vu of professional insta-bility and my daughter's war with socks. What matters, though, what is urgent, is that I am alone in a log cabin with a wild animal who has to put on clothes.

"*Putain*, Nina, Mama has to *go!*"

There it is, the first spout of lava. My husband is French, so when I swear in front of our daughter, I coat bad words in this foreign language, hoping it will soften their impact. Nina's face reddens and her concentrated lips tremble: the landing wasn't soft. I need to back off. I don't.

"Dammit, Nina, if you could just get the damn socks on! Go barefoot! I can't take it! Mama has to *go!*"

Nina's dimpled hands drop to her sides. Her face collapses. She begins to sob. My heart divides: one half wants to get down and hold her, apologize for the fact that she has an impatient, desperate mother; the other wants to hurl fire from my mouth, wants to scream so loud it scares her, wants the battle of attrition with the socks and the zippers and the tomato sauce to stop.

I wrap my arms around my daughter and lift her struggling limbs into the air, my muscles straining against the fury of her temper tantrum. Grasping her shoes and shoving them under my armpit, I walk out of the house like this, my boots crunching on the autumn frost as Nina tries to kick me. I will drive her to day care barefoot. We will try again in the parking lot. We will try again.

•

"Have you taken a depression intake survey before?" asks the fledgling therapist I have chosen from a list of local providers on the World Wide Web, apparently erroneously, because there is no way I can bare my soul to a twentysomething in a Livestrong bracelet. Even his name—Joe—seems incongruous with the bookish sophistication I'd fantasized a therapist possessing. I shift in the plush seat that holds me like a velvet clam. Somewhere behind me, a white noise machine hisses a eucalyptus scent.

"I don't know," I answer. "I don't think so?" I look down at the sheet of questions. Father's parenting style, mother's parenting style, religious upbringing. My stomach clenches. "Or maybe once? My parents sent me to a therapist when they got divorced. Or my mother did. My mother made me."

"And you were how old?"

"Nine."

I watch him do the math: the patient who's in front of him is thirty-seven now. *See how long I stayed in working order for,* I want to say, *before the "check engine" light came on?*

He leaves the room so I can fill out the form in private. It is a long form, thick with pages. Thick with questions I would like to laugh at, but can't.

Significant childhood experiences
Good/happy/positive Age Bad/negative/sad/disturbing Age

————————— —— —————————— ——

————————— —— —————————— ——

The questions are difficult to answer, too difficult and big. It is absurd, the hugeness of these questions staring up at me. They are something hard dressed up as something easy, like the password reminders that come at you out of nowhere on a Tuesday demanding the name of the best friend you ditched in elementary school, the name of your first street.

I flip to the second page, where I navigate questions about my sleep, which is nonexistent. Do I feel bad about myself? Do I feel like I am a failure and/or have let my family down? If I have little interest and pleasure in doing things, do I experience these feelings: Nearly every day? More than half the days? Do I have trouble concentrating? Do I have thoughts of hurting myself?

"The trees want me to drive into them" isn't an option on the intake form, so I answer "Nearly every day," instead. The therapist comes back into the scented office, and it's my turn to leave the room while he evaluates my answers in the whir of his white lair. When I come back in, he's flushed. The chair holds me even tighter. He tells me that my answers are the answers of someone with a severe case of depression. Is there someone who can escort me home? He doesn't think that I should drive.

•

At thirty-seven, I did not know what depression looked like, but I refused to admit that it could look like me: a woman with a mortgage and a helpful husband and a healthy child and a beloved family pet buried in the yard. That I felt sadness was undeniable, but I felt no right to claim it. My sadness was like an abandoned case shouldering around the black wrap of a baggage belt. How I wanted to pretend that it was someone else's baggage. Depression? Not my depression. Can't happen to me.

But the despair was fully mine. It kept me from absorbing nutrients. It sat on my chest at night. For months I had been suffering from an insomnia so debilitating that I'd moved into the guest room so that Leo could do the thing I hated and envied him for: sleep.

I had been at my happiest at thirty-five. That age was right behind me. An age where I could stare into my daughter's face all day and bleep and squint and gurgle back at her own gurgles, revel at the makeup of her kneecap, the fact that she had hands. Put as much care into the pureeing of beets as I did into the plotting of a novel; tick off the list of "must-haves" for a car ride with the attention of a surgeon general.

But when Nina turned two, everything changed. Her needs became vast and existential: no longer did I tower over her disgruntlements wondering, Is she hot? Hungry? Too cold? All of a sudden, she wanted entertainment. She wanted meaning, reason, proof. Nina wanted a form of love that was far beyond the planned care I'd shown up until that point. *Look at how I love you because I provide* needed to turn into *look at how I love you because I am dropping everything to play*, and at thirty-seven, I did not know how to play, because somehow, my ability to be comfortable in joy had left my heart and body.

On the way home from that first visit to the therapist's, the trees didn't beckon me to drive outside the dividing lines. Instead, I saw my mother's finger on a map of South Carolina, a game we used to play when we were in the summer house that my father didn't come to anymore. We would stand at the dining room table with our eyes closed, my mother's right hand out. I'd spin her around twice, and she'd drop her finger somewhere on the map. Large city or small city, in the middle of everything or nowhere, it didn't matter, we would drive there. Car snacks and water bottles were the extent of our planning. We'd get in the car and we would drive, and when we got to the spot that her finger had selected on the map, we would find a place to eat lunch, and then we would head back. It would take all day, sometimes, these spontaneous explorations. I don't remember us having heart-to-heart talks on our miniature road trips, although I do remember my mother trying to protect me from disappointment by laughing if we discovered that our destination was a one-horse town with nothing but a Sunoco and a shuttered Laundromat. One time, we landed in a speck of a town called Aynor, "Population 490," according to a rudimentary placard lodged near a stop sign. There wasn't anything in Aynor then: no diner to eat eggs in, not even a gas station where we could get a bag of chips. I was suddenly deflated by my mother's fallibility: she'd made a mistake in the place her finger chose, we were going to be hungry, this would not be fun. Then my mother nodded as if she had resolved something. "Four hundred ninety-two now!" she shouted at the sign. She revealed she'd stuffed the cooler full of potato chips and turkey sandwiches just in case, and we sat on a beach towel in front of the town sign to eat our picnic. My mother was like that: pragmatic so that she could be flexible. Those drives—ample, countless—were my mother showing me that distraction can be healing, that fun is medication, that you can drive away from anything that hurts.

I need one of those drives now: an escape from my own self. But my mind is so muddled with sleeplessness, I don't know where to go. I have tried alcohol and acting out and kissing other men. I have tried acupuncture and exercise, no exercise, essential oils, drugs made in a lab. I have tried denial. None of this makes me sleep, and without sleep, I have no boundaries: I am not a writer mother wife, I am a blob, struggling through the hours with eyes that will not close.

There are pastures on my way home from the therapist's white office. Though my horse life is thirty years behind me, my brain turns to equines. In my mind, I smell wet hay and touch dry muzzle, consider silver moss in the Beaufort County oak tree I was under when I had my final fall. In Irish folk custom, there is a Celtic goddess named Epona who reigns over fertility, horses, and the powers of the mind. Dressed in black, she appears at daybreak bearing nightmares at a point where four roads cross. Her horse is always white. It makes sense, this color, I think, trying to keep my mind on the road and the turns that I must take. In ancient times, the movements of white horses were interpreted as auguries: if a horse crossed over a specific battle line with its left foot instead of its right one, if it neighed before or after the others in the cavalry, war was started or war was set aside—the rider of the neighing horse did, or didn't, charge.

A combination, perhaps, of superstition and reverence, white steeds influenced felicity, as well. During the Iron Age on the green hills now known as Uffington, prehistoric people dug trenches in the form of a running horse and filled them with white chalk. Visible from the heavens, the horse functioned as a kind of bat-signal, beseeching higher powers to cart the sun across the sky.

Driving home to a husband who will want to hear whether therapy is going to help me, to a daughter who will smell of milk and Goldfish crackers and whom it will take forty minutes to coerce into a bath, I think that I will take a white horse or a black one, anything that will help me face sundown with less dread.

2

ROCKING HORSE

The first horse I ever saw was a dappled gray Pegasus with anime blue eyes and silver feathering around her jolly hooves. Her name was Flutterby, and she was the creation of an illustrator, Robin James, and a writer, Stephen Cosgrove, in a book by the same name.

Before becoming obsessed with *Flutterby*, the story of a winged horse who wasn't sure what her job was on the island of Serendipity, I was obsessed with her conformation. I swooned at her rump's roundness, her haughty hooves and shiny fetlocks: those delicate dips where the cannon bone of a horse's leg meets its sloping pastern. And her nostrils! Shaped like quotation marks but prone to blow open in frustration when she'd suffered yet another humiliation (she tried to work with the busy ants on Serendipity, she tried working with the bees), they huffed and puffed with indignity as Flutterby sought her raison d'être among her fellow creatures. That Flutterby eventually realized that she was only meant to be herself was a message I cared not two whits about when I was tiny: Ponies could fly! They had tufts of mane that bounced over their ears so charmingly! Horses liked to play!

It was 1983 in Greenwich, Connecticut, where I was born and raised. I was five years old, and unlike listless Flutterby, I knew my job in life: it was to go to my first year of real school—an all-girls school called Greenwich Academy—pay attention to the teacher, and have the biggest, brightest, cleanest Trapper Keeper fresh out of Lisa Frank.

All the designs that romped over the must-have binders and school organizers of the 1980s featured white horses, just like my dear Flutterby. Sometimes they were winged with spiraling horns, always they had rainbow manes and neon, hot-pink hooves. The world of Lisa Frank was positively vibrating with glee and possibility: a cosmology born out of the free-spirited antics of Punky Brewster, Pippi Longstocking, and Anne of Green Gables, my sisters in arms when I was a child, the girls who taught me that it was better to create a pony out of a stick and jump it over a berry bush than to cry because you didn't have the thing you wanted.

Which was, for me, a horse. As I grew in mind and height, my annual supplications to Santa Claus went from pretty-pretty-pleases for this or that new Breyer horse to hand-scrawled petitions for an actual, live pony (preferably one that was white with a steel-gray mane, thank you very much). When Santa didn't deliver, I tried writing the tooth fairy, and when that didn't pan out, I tried sweet-talking my mother, who was clearly in charge of whatever gifts I unwrapped for my birthday.

My fifth Christmas arrived with five times the usual fanfare. Christmas has always been my mother's favorite holiday, but that season, she was pregnant: it would be our last holiday as a family of three. She went all out: a real tree in my bedroom as well as in my parents'. Wreaths and potted poinsettia and tiny Christmas lights, a nativity on the mantel made out of painted wood.

My bedroom was on the second floor of our home, and per family tradition, I wasn't allowed to get out of bed until I felt a lump above my toes, a knitted, bulging stocking deposited by Santa at some point in the night.

Then, I'd sit bolt upright and could open just one present before running into my parents' bedroom to let them know that Santa had, indeed, come through.

My mother would run up a tray of toast and juice and coffee and we'd clamber into bed to rifle through our individual stockings together: mint ChapSticks for my father, tiny jams for me, small soaps the color of grass in summer, pens with horse charms dangling off them, and heart-shaped school erasers. After that quick breakfast, it was time for the big reveal. My mother would hold my hand as I walked down the staircase that led into the great hall where the fragrant Christmas tree would have been standing guard all through December. But this time, I encountered something unexpected. It wasn't wrapped, and it wasn't underneath the tree so much as blocking it: something massive, horse-sized, under a white sheet.

It couldn't be a horse; I was old enough to realize this. The object didn't move and it didn't smell. But it was very big. "Go ahead and open it," my mother coaxed me, which meant that I had permission to yank off the white sheet.

It was a horse! It was! A horse of wood and shine! A rocking horse the size of an actual, large pony, with real stirrups and a real bit and—lovelier still—leather reins that you could hold as the horse bounded out of the house and into the fields beyond, which were not fields, really, but neighbors, which didn't matter one iota because we could ride up on the neighbors' roofs and fly into the sky.

In the velour dressing gown my mother liked me to go to bed in on December 24, I climbed up into the saddle and we promptly discovered that this behemoth of mahogany weighed more than a Clydesdale and was impossible to rock. My mother had to plant herself behind me and push forward and backward with all her might to make me move. But no matter. Just like with any horse, I would have to get stronger, better, fearless, and then I'd be able to ride off on my own.

•

My best friend at the time was a sunny child named Kristin, flaxen-haired and smiling, with the milky complexion of the Dutch. We were inseparable as children, immersed in worlds of our own making.

Though Kristin's thing was singing, she was patient and forgiving, so I pushed the horses on her. My backyard, the kingdom of our weekends, became a Grand Prix course of poles and trials and water jumps, which necessitated leaping from a stone bench to the bank of our small pond without slipping or getting our hooves caked in mud. My paternal grandmother—imported for most weekends from nearby Tarrytown—shone in her position as our eventing judge, immaculately dressed as her Southern upbringing demanded, poker-faced during our exertions, pausing before the presentation of the scores she'd written on the perforated paper from the electric typewriter that my father never used.

It would be mine in a year's time, his office and his desk, also, as he spent more and more time away from home and I learned to read and write. Even today, the sight of dot matrix printing paper brings back the thrill of creating my first stories in a room with a closed door.

On our playdates that stretched throughout the weekend, Kristin and I would write songs together on my electronic keyboard if the weather wasn't good. If it was nice, we were outside. Toppled bikes and lemonade stands and bubble wands fill my mind alongside the crossrails we created out of broomsticks for the horses that we were. Playing outside was invigorating and inspirational, but it was also practical: the insides of my house weren't so pleasant anymore. After my brother's birth, family time was ice time, conversations were slippery, there was a spreading crack. Outside, outside, outside, though, the world was full of brighter, safer worlds. Caterpillars and butterflies, quick snakes in the grass, and acorn-stuffed chipmunks with cheeks chubbier than mine. We chartered fishing expeditions by that pond of ours, and I remember Kristin wasn't squeamish about worms: she seemed to like the wet feel of them between her fingers, the way they'd wriggle on the line once she got them hooked. Though I liked sitting beside her, waiting to see if anything would chomp, I hated the worm business. I was always a fur person: a person who liked mammals. To this day I am terrified by things that don't have eyes, perhaps because watching and observing is how I make sense of the world.

And my world was changing: my father's relationship to my brother wasn't what it had been with baby me. I remember being held by Daddy, pulled sleeping from the car. He took me to lunch at the top of the World Trade Center where he worked, he let me order filet mignon and swiss roll cake, beaming in front of the waiters when they came to take our plates and saw that I'd cleared mine. My mother was proud of telling people that I was the only child let into the Union League Club in Manhattan: my father had assured the protesting maître d' of that private supper club that I'd be on my best behavior, and I always was. Daddy's little girl, I accompanied him in the beginning on business trips to Palm Springs and Hawaii. Looking back now, I'm not sure where the business part came into these trips, but I do remember his leather briefcase and calls on hotel phones. Back home, he was there for me—home each day by seven; a tide of Polo by Ralph Lauren cologne swept into the front hall. I would run to meet him every evening like a child in a storybook, except this storybook isn't fictional: it's the way my daughter greets me now.

I was six when Santa came around again, a Santa who had been the recipient of a dozen missives that year about how much I liked my rocking horse, but the prettiest of pleases, could I have a real pony? I would take beautiful care of him. It was all I'd ever ask for, it was all I'd ever need. When our stocking breakfast was more substantial than usual because my dad said that we'd have to go on a drive to see my present, my stomach lurched: I had got my wish.

The pony was waiting for me in Bedford, a land of horse fences and named barns in neighboring New York. There were bales of hay wrapped inside white plastic dotting the landscape like small igloos. With every farm we passed, I felt more sure, my heart beating inside of me like something about to tear through a cocoon.

A rote hello to someone and then there he was: a brown pony on crossties with a big red bow around his neck, a pony the color of rubbed leather and fresh straw with a wild lion mane that bounced about and tufts of white around his hooves: he could have been white, he could have been purple—it didn't matter, he was mine.

I named my pony Fantasy, and if I hadn't needed my mother to get me there in a motor vehicle, I would have been in that barn all the time. To this day, when I'm feeling low or under the weather, I look up pictures of the rudimentary beds some dedicated owners have built above their horses' stalls, thinking how lucky they are to share the darkness with the snuffles and the nickers and the rustlings of a horse.

After that fateful purchase, it was ponies all the time. I had ponies on my Trapper Keepers, I drew ponies on my school assignments—when I went to sleep at night, I would imagine the smell of my pony's hair, conjure up the way it felt to braid his mane and tail, the satisfying *plop* of dirt scraped from a hoof. Fantasy was my imagination's complement and a real form of escape. I started jumping nearly as soon as I was put on him: in horsey circles, Fantasy was known as a "push-button pony," which means you could point him at a Volvo and he'd jump right over it.

Loyal to my passions, Kristin started coming with me to horse shows, our Friday-night sleepovers cut short by a four o'clock alarm: me, Kristin, and my little brother rolled into the Wagoneer with the turkey-and-mayo sandwiches my mother fixed at the kitchen island while the car heated outside.

Away we went from the house each weekend, farther and farther afield. My father, where was Dad? He golfed, he played tennis, his Wall Street business trips extended. It was always my mother who took me to the barn, not just for weekend horse shows but for lessons and ring time during the week as well. The drive out after school was beautiful, but long. For me, the drive there was anticipatory (How would I perform that day? How high would I jump?) and reflective on the way back (I'd had only one refusal at a crossrail, but I could do better next time). For my mother, though, those drives were simply long. She wanted to talk, surely. She's always been someone who is comforted by chit-chat, whereas in the car especially, I like to sit inside my thoughts. At six years old, I didn't think of my mother's comfort. I didn't think that it was cold inside the barn if you weren't grooming or feeding or riding on a horse, or that it was lonely for her while I faced down crossrails and laughed with the young riders. My mother was my joy-mobile. It was her job to drive me to the thing that made me happy, that was what I thought, and because she kept on driving me—never with a protest, never put me in a carpool—that was what I continued to think until my parents called a meeting by our pool one day when I was eight and my brother four, and announced that my father was moving out, that they were divorcing.

Now, of course, I look back on those barn trips differently: all those silent car rides, the many hours my mother was alone with her own thoughts, which were not good thoughts, were thoughts of the "What do I do now?" variety, or "How much should I take him for?" and "What did I do wrong?" Not that my mother would have had a confidant about her husband's infidelities in a six-year-old, but I'm ashamed that I was deaf to her suffering, that I thought (resolutely, giddily) only of myself.

My mother, I know now, was frightened of horses. I don't remember her ever getting on one, and she was always behind a gate or on the bleachers when I rode. For most people there are only two reactions when it comes to horses: fear that fascinates or fear that repels. My mom fell into the latter camp, especially when I graduated from the pint-sized Fantasy to the sixteen-hands-high Woody, a flea-bitten gray (as such coloring is referred to) with a flair for drama and a restless head. And when I started jumping higher and falling with more regularity, horses became a fire that needed putting out.

I would stop riding at nine years old, a year after my brother started having the seizures that would plague him his entire childhood, until he had a defibrillator put in to control his wild heart. The barn, already a forty-minute drive from our family home, became an hour away when my mother, brother, and I moved to a new house in Old Greenwich. I was circling a different set of friends by then, the popular girls, the ones whose Friday-night sleepovers earned you social status, events I couldn't attend if I had to be in jodhpurs and plaited hair by the crack of Saturday.

"What if you took a break from it?" my mother asked. "Just a break, a year? If you want to go back to riding after that, we'll find a way to make it work."

It was true that riding made it difficult to gain traction with the cool kids. Barn time meant I couldn't get on the prank calls that my new friends orchestrated from their private lines on conference call, that I couldn't linger at the dismissal area with a Snapple and giggle about boys, that I couldn't participate in the Friday ballroom-dancing classes that were the only way for us girls' school students to interact with boys. Fine, I'd take a break,

I said, acting as if this were a great sacrifice, as if the fact that I had to make a sacrifice were my grieving mother's fault. Fantasy, whom I always thought was "mine," had actually been a rental, long since leased out to another lucky girl. Now Woody was to follow. My jodhpurs and show shirts were put into a tack trunk bearing my initials, my black velvet helmet with the grosgrain ribbon, too. This trunk was put in the garage of my father's new house in Greenwich where his large dogs would later gnaw on it. I would not get on a horse again until I was thirty-eight years old.

3

ARTAX

The horse that I love above all others is drowning in a swamp. The sucking mud is up to his legs now, his immaculate white coat sullied, his nostrils huge with terror. His young master, Atreyu, tugs on the reins, yanking with all his force in the direction of dry land, but to no avail. It's like Artax is in quicksand, if sand were black as dark.

"Artax," screams the disbelieving hero, "what's the matter?! . . . ARTAX!"

In the film version of *The NeverEnding Story*, Atreyu's faithful steed doesn't talk, but in the book, he does.

"With every step we take," the horse answers, "the sadness grows in my heart. I've lost hope, master. And I feel so heavy, so heavy. I can't go on!"

In the mythical land of Fantasia that they're navigating, Atreyu and his horse both know that to stop in the Swamps of Sadness is to give in to the sadness: you get stuck and then you die. Desperate in front of his friend's passiveness, Atreyu shouts at his horse to believe, to go on because they must go on, to choose life over stasis. But his horse—a white horse that looks just like my Flutterby—is too defeated to choose life.

The film version of *The NeverEnding Story* was so popular upon its release in 1984 that many parents must have assumed, as mine did, that the movie was perfectly acceptable for children to watch unchaperoned. Accordingly, many people of my generation took in life's most gruesome lessons across one minute and forty seconds alone. Your best friends can abandon you, everything you love will change, the being you love the most will eventually die.

The obvious lesson that the Swamps of Sadness episode carries about depression was too adult for me to grasp the first time that I watched it, squirreled away in the second-story guest room that hadn't seen guests in it for a long time. How could anyone let this happen to Atreyu, and us children? The horse would come back, wouldn't he? Horses couldn't *die*. Your best friend wouldn't choose surrender over a happy life together, frolicking in fields? The film's end credits were amended to have Atreyu galloping across the verdant lands of Fantasia on a resurrected pony, so visceral was the backlash from parents whose children were emotionally changed after witnessing the Swamps of Sadness scene. I didn't run to my mother after Artax perished—I didn't tell her it couldn't be possible that the horse had drowned, could she hit rewind? In any case, I don't remember my mother being there when I watched and rewatched it: she walked a lot with her girlfriends, then, ate a lot of lunches. My father was always playing tennis or golf at some country club. My parents needed adult time to buttress their failing marriage. My father had a car phone then, which made me think that he was Knight Rider and his car was KITT, but I remember it ringing and ringing when I hoped he would pick up.

And so it was that I held on to my complicated feelings about that movie all alone: how much I loved Atreyu, how much I loved his horse, how much I believed in his quest to find the Childlike Empress and to give her a new name so that Fantasia would be saved from the vapid enemy, the Nothing. In my mind, that sadness is the first big secret that I kept from my mother, a secret that grew larger and more powerful the more I watched the movie and started to grasp what the Swamps of Sadness stood for.

I was eight years old when insomnia first leaked in around my feet, rising in a slow tide that would eventually submerge me. I had seasons of bad nights behind me at that point: my second-floor bedroom wasn't the safe place I ran down from to meet real Christmas trees anymore; it was the perch from which I could hear my parents accusing one another of various betrayals, the car engine turning over, hear the icebox open and open yet again. Then there'd be my little brother crying, needing Mother's care. He was smaller than I was, he hadn't had the cushy years that I'd had: summer trips with Daddy present, the skyscraper I knew intimately as the place where our dad worked. Although I longed for someone to confide in during those scary nights, I felt that my worries would be a bother if I shared them, one more weight upon a house whose foundation was friable.

My insomnia entered my life then in the form that it still haunts me with today: I'm able to fall asleep at night, but I wake up too early, utterly unable to squire myself back to sleep at 3:00 or 4:00 AM. My current coping mechanisms—leave the bed, nibble on an Ambien, read somewhere with my book light until I fall asleep—are less selfish than they were when I was eight. I had two twin beds in my childhood bedroom; mine was covered in a bevy of stuffed animals. After having spent too many a sleepover spiraling into the frightening solitude of being the only mind awake, I started to use these "stuffies" as tactical pawns. Once dawn broke, I would toss a stuffed animal at the other body in my bedroom, and if my aim wasn't true, I'd strike again until my confused sleepover guest woke up, groggy, sure that something had hit her, still rubbing her eyes as I agreed that that was so weird, but as long as she was awake, did she want to play?

My anxiety at the time was architectural in form: my childhood home, a fairyland stone Tudor, had been the birthplace of all the games I played with my friends and the stories I made up: hallowed ground for me. I started writing things when I was seven, and by the time I was eight years old, all my stories dealt with a little girl who is about to lose her home. In one of these stapled manuscripts ("The Magic Rose Bush," indicates my kiddie pencil), a girl flees her house when she hears a real estate agent talking about how her parents are going to sell it. Outside, she cries upon a rosebush, and her tears activate a secret staircase that leads her to an underworld filled with an alternative family of animals, where—even though the girl realizes that her parents will miss her—she decides to stay.

I became obsessed with secret underworlds that permitted escape under the moonlight. I could spend hours daydreaming about the twelve dancing princesses who fugue through a trapdoor in their bedroom to a golden-leafed lagoon that winds around a castle, where they dance illicitly into the night's cold hours; the labyrinth of waterways under the Parisian opera house in *The Phantom of the Opera* preoccupied me for years; the fact that a sixteen-year-old wished her brother into goblin form and had only thirteen hours to find him in a maze lest he stay a monster forever seemed less like the movie *Labyrinth* and more like a manifestation of my darkest thoughts, to me.

If I had stayed with the horse riding, my fantastical obsessions could have seen me painting my horses' hooves with glitter and braiding colored string through manes at best; at worst, I might have morphed into a horse worshipper straight out of *Equus*, sneaking into barns to ride horses naked under stars. But with horse escape behind me, I took to my father's typewriter in his emptied study, where I built worlds of my own. I had three stories and then I had five and then I had more and more of them. One day in art class, a trusted teacher, Mrs. Vicidomini, showed us students how to make book jacket covers out of floral wallpaper and where to include an "About the Author" section, and that was it: writing became less of a career goal than a dream already activated. I would be a writer, there was no other path.

The other day, I hosted an event for an author I much admire via Zoom, as all author interviews are conducted during the pandemic I'm writing from. I asked this author—who writes about contemporary anxieties: the endangered planet, the endangered female body—how she mines anxiety-producing topics without writing anxious prose. I was embarrassed by her answer, because it proved I'd shown my cards. "I don't write for catharsis," she said. "I don't write from or through a place of anxiety. I write when I am calm."

I envied her relationship to writing, just as I felt myself cleaving away from the writer I so admired. So we're a different species of writer then, I thought, as I smiled into the screen where attendees I couldn't see were watching. I wrote to keep on moving through the Swamps of Sadness. I started writing to keep happiness inside.

4

THE DEAD ZONE

It is day three in a house that we have rented with eighteen of my husband's French friends; six of these are children. The house, more of a château, is in the South of France and sounded like paradise when we booked it for this August 2015 respite: a stone castle, cypress trees, an in-ground, shaded pool. In reality, the land is cracked from heat and fly-infested, the store is a twenty-minute drive, and most of my husband's Paris-born friends don't have licenses, putting Leo and me on the short list of people who drive back and forth into town for never-ending bread and groceries day part after day part: early morning, late morning, late afternoon. When we are not shopping or cooking or cleaning up the food that we have cooked, we are on recreation deathwatch: the pool's tiled deck is slick as ice when wet, and with so many people coming in and out of the water, the deck is always wet. We start adding bandages and first-aid tape to grocery lists to soothe the children's falls.

For the weeklong trip to Cévennes, I packed caftans and a wide-brimmed hat that I stole from my mother's closet when I last visited her in Florida. I have paperbacks and sunblock, diapers and backup pacifiers; pacifiers are the only way our child falls asleep. Despite the crushing pressure of a September book deadline, a growing tumor in my marriage that keeps us from so much as hugging, and the venom of insomnia snaking through my blood, I agreed to this vacation: I agreed that time around easygoing people would bring me ease as well.

But I'm not feeling easy: proximity to the happy-go-lucky isn't helping me. My long-held conviction that it's risky to relax had been proven accurate a month earlier, right before we left for France. On the way to the Hartford Bradley airport from our home in the southern Berkshires, a car cut across our right-of-way and my husband, who was driving, couldn't brake in time. The force of the impact with the other driver sent us—my husband and a friend of ours who was going to shepherd our car home in the front seats; me, my daughter, and a dusty bag of Cheerios in the back—across the opposite lane into a tree. The airbags exploded, the car's hood accordioned, our little car was totaled. Physically, aside from some seat-belt burns and bruises, we were okay, but mentally, the accident was a match to the depression that would engulf me by summer's end.

My husband and I have different memories of that accident: Leo thought the other driver (who was exiting a strip mall) saw us and had come to a full stop, and thus we could continue traveling safely at our current speed. I remember looking up from the plastic bag of cereal I was portioning for Nina, noting the driver who seemed to be *thinking* about stopping at the upcoming intersection without really committing to it, and assuming that Leo would slow down out of caution. On paper and off, the other driver was at fault, as the police report would attest, but the accident unleashed a treasonous contaminant; a chemical chain of doubt. If I had been driving, would the accident have happened? I think the worst of people, while Leo thinks the best of them. Therefore, I would have slowed.

A conviction cemented in the days after the accident: the defensive way I lived and mothered, was, in fact, of use. By the time we arrived in Cévennes, I had stopped sleeping completely. My nervous system crackled with electric snaps. My skin turned grayish, my posture stooped. My eyes dulled from the French sleeping pills that couldn't override my brain's decision to stay up and at the ready.

Whether it was an aside from my husband or the stress radiating from my person that landed us this prize, Nina, Leo, and I get the nicest room in the château: a turret complete with red velvet curtains and a desk where I can finish the novel that is due in just six weeks. We're supplied with an antique crib for Nina courtesy of the castle's owner, a wrought-iron antique placed squatly at the foot of our shared bed. We've never slept in the same room with our daughter: Nina's been in her own room since we tried room sharing post-hospital; her lively body tossed and turned so much, we opted for the video monitor and a crib downstairs. Nina's heavier now; her turns make the crib screech. The crib has giant slats through which everything falls: her favorite bunny, the pacifier she needs to stay in a deep sleep. The splat of the pacifier on wood is a sound I wait for, so I can retrieve the sucker before she wakes in rage. I stay awake despite the sleeping pills: vigilant, prepared. With all the turning and the creaking of exhausted bedsprings, Leo doesn't sleep much either.

Rinse and rinse, repeat. Our days in Cévennes are a fog of fly swatting and dish washing and the spinning of a chore wheel that somebody's fiancée has drawn up: a girl who sleeps through her own chores because she's the only one who's childless, descending into our parenting chaos with eyes puffy from sleep, a girl who walks by the mounting dishes to the driveway, holding her phone aloft in search of network bars. After lunch, she retires to her bedroom for a nap, and I hate her youthful lustiness, the lover of her sleep. I want what she has: REM sleep and the sex I imagine happening on her side of the castle. I'm so untouched by rest and adult skin that I cook up a fantasy involving a dilapidated chapel I discover one day on a run through the dry woods. I churn up a whole scene around the structure, a local mason hired to restore it to its former glory, an offering of water from a cool well for my sweating body, a daytime bout of need in the shade of that old chapel, a signal to my untouched self that I haven't lost it yet, that I can still incite desire in someone other than myself.

The truth is that Leo would have been there for me if I'd reached for him, would have reciprocated if I'd found the courage to ask him to reach for me. But I'd shored my ego with the lore of self-sufficiency for too long to risk revealing that I needed someone else. So I stomped on alone, convinced that meeting my daily word count was more important than my health, that handing in my book on time might actually save my marriage.

I wish that I'd been less destroyed in Cévennes that summer—more available, more *there*. There was an old friend of my husband's on that trip, a handsome Frenchman with the improbable name of Lenny, a guy who had been diagnosed with depression a year earlier, had had to go to a hospital, was laid off from his job.

He spent that entire week lurking around the property sucking on an electronic cigarette with a small, moist sound. I did not see him as a fellow soldier (when I asked Leo why Lenny had been hospitalized, he said that it had been a shock for him to become a father, *devenir un père*); instead, I saw him as inscrutable, a prisoner of his mind. As for me, my problems were all work-related. Writing had been my solace and my moneymaker for so long that having the writing founder was incredibly shameful. I thought I was miserable because I owed my editor a second novel and the manuscript was awful; I would have been outraged had someone suggested that my struggles to get my book right were related to my failings as a parent. Even though my every hour was filled with exasperation and a sense of helplessness around my daughter, I remained convinced that I had motherhood under control. I was maniacal about balanced meals and nap times; Nina's clothes bore hand-stitched name tags, her nails were clipped, and she had lovely books to read. If there was trouble in my home life, it was only in my marriage, that I would have copped to, but as a parent, I was sterling.

I look back and I feel softness for the woman who packed aspirational outfits for the mother she wanted to be on that vacation: joyful and available, gauzy with pink drink but devoted to her daughter, charming, a languid touch on the nape of her bent husband. I wanted to be kind. I wasn't. Looking back with the lens of years between me and that arid property, I see now that I wasn't able to vacation because I'd cut myself off from the possibility that a family could bring joy. Work brought joy, and because the writing wasn't going well, there could be no joy.

I missed my book deadline that September, the first time I'd ever missed a deadline in my Virgo life. The self-sufficiency fable I had spun had let me through its gaps, and I was falling with no parachute above me and no safety net below.

5

BLACK HORSE

FAMINE

I walked the carpeted hallway toward the principal's office, the headquarters of a woman I had done my damnedest to avoid since I had broken up my friendship with her daughter, Kristin, the year before.

I was a different person now, thin and *European*, a change I was working hard to signal that day in the short-sleeved, ribbed turtleneck and brown pumps I'd "picked up" in Spain at a chain retailer that had seemed, to eighth-grade me, like an haute-couture emporium of elegance and glamour.

My new best friend, Rebecca, had moved to Madrid for one year and I'd spent the summer with her family, including one month in Barcelona for the 1992 Olympics. It was in Spain that I first experienced the intoxicating calm that can come over you if you make it past the hunger pains and long delay a meal.

We were on a Spanish schedule that entire summer: breakfast at 10:30, lunch in the 4:00 PM range, dinner around 10:00. It was so hot between breakfast and lunch, there wasn't anything more sensible to do than gossip and return to bed: I remember Rebecca's rental home had military-grade blinds that shut out the mere idea of natural light. On ironed sheets in the pitch black, we would sleep the catatonic rest of adolescence, our dreams filled with the possibilities of our post-lunch snack, when Rebecca's mother would let us walk into the city chaperoned by Rebecca's older sister to get an ice cream cone.

It was on these snack excursions that I first noticed women's bodies in a way I never had before. My girls' school was a uniformed one, plaid kilts and solid-colored tops, and the time I spent envying other people's attributes there was devoted exclusively to the thick and perfect ponytails that were the trademark of the cool girls. I myself had thin hair, straight and mousy letdowns that I used children's barrettes to tame because my hair wasn't thick enough to keep an adult-sized barrette in place.

Hair type, the clearness of a complexion versus ruddy, freckled mine, this was where my comparisons to other girls in my class stopped, but in Spain, I couldn't stop admiring the female form in full. Lynxlike in gait and purpose, the women of Spain's capital didn't seem to walk so much as saunter, scarved and bloused and turned out like show ponies headed for the ring.

And they were so *lean*. Even the young girls my age seemed stretched out to ballerina proportions, like gum caught between branches. With the exception of Rebecca, who was gymnast-petite, my friends and I were pudgy, dimpled of knee and elbow, our faces rounded by bagels and Fruit Roll-Ups; tall and strong were some of us, but none of us were lean.

There was something to this leanness I stood gaping at in the boulevards of summertime Madrid. It was commanding and fluid—these señoritas had allure. I wanted to move through time and space as they did: the self-possession with which they raised a grapefruit to their nostrils, contemplated a roll of paper towels, as if the commonest of errands could not dampen the proof that they were loved.

That was the summer that I started up with Grape-Nuts, a hearty cereal made of wheat-and-barley nuggets that was filling and low-fat. I remember being introduced to them by Rebecca's Spanish housekeeper, though this seems incongruous to me: Were Post brand cereals available in Spain? She had a particular way of serving them: a single heaping spoonful of Grape-Nuts set in a low dish of milk, like something you might feed a favored stray cat in the streets. I was hungry—it wasn't enough breakfast— but it seemed that to ask for seconds from this woman would be American and gauche, so over the course of my first week there, I made peace with that hunger until it became a bulwark against my decadence: my oh-so-American need to be secure and overfed.

I think it was the second week in Spain that I started swimming in Rebecca's pool, not for fun, for laps. I started with fifty, then it was one hundred every day. One hundred laps after a spoonful of Grape-Nuts and a plate of melon and ham for lunch. Maybe I wouldn't have kept up with the swimming and the sinking into hunger if I hadn't seen results so quickly: in mere days, it seemed, I was sinuous, gazelle-like, elongated and slimmed.

In Barcelona, it was hotter: pastel sherbets and cold fish salads were the only appetizing options as the mercury continued to climb. The sun beat down all the time on us, even in the boxed Olympic seats that had come as a perk with Rebecca's father's job. Muscles, muscles all around me; it was the summer of the body. I became ill once in the grandstand while watching the men's hundred-meter dash: it was well over a hundred degrees that day, and nothing solid had passed my lips since the nuggets in thin milk. Rebecca's sister took me for an ice cream sandwich from the amphitheater's snack stand and I remember vowing that I would swim the calories off the following morning.

I wasn't actively unhappy with the body I had then—I didn't want to punish it or anything like that. Except for my thin hair, which I loathed and was embarrassed by, I was tall and had long legs, I liked the color of my eyes, I liked my physical casing more or less just fine. But I wanted to transmit *difference*. Some kind of intelligence or superciliousness that I could signal physically, a figure that people would look at and think, This is a girl apart. It started out like that, a desire for a style change, the way a teen might move from jock to goth or prep to skater; I just wanted to be different. And then, when it went on long enough, as for most anorexics, my relationship to eating became about control.

I was getting away with something when I came back in September. I saw girls whispering near lockers, and my mother surely said something to me when I was handed over to her at JFK Airport, a "You look so different!" probably, that I shut down with a glare. But nobody confronted me about the weight I'd lost, pounds and pounds of it, not my father or his new wife, not my ponytailed girlfriends. Nobody said a thing. Nobody until I was called in before lunch one day to see the middle school principal, mother of my ex-friend.

The shame I felt in my belly while walking there tricks my mind into remembering that long carpeted hallway as soggy and wet, but it wasn't of course, it was vacuumed daily, although I do remember that the day was humid, with August right behind us. Because Kristin and I had never had it out about our friend breakup, I thought this was the face-off, I thought that her mother was going to take me to task for leaving her daughter behind for a clique of rich kids, and I didn't know if I would cry or feel sicker to my stomach when and if she said this.

I was so embarrassed when I reached Principal H.'s office that I could barely talk. I remember that I felt small in the chair across from hers, and silly in my shoes with a small heel, my beatnik top a posture for the woman who had seen all my pajamas, whose daughter slept in my guest bed as often as her own.

"We've had some concerns," Principal H. started. "Some people are concerned about your weight loss. You're getting very thin."

Was I already a vegetarian, or was that something I invented on the spot that day and then had to adhere to because it was such an easy answer to a darker question? Did I say that I was swimming? Because I wasn't swimming anymore. I didn't have the energy to: I was skipping lunch and using a morning bowl of Grape-Nuts to stand in for two meals. Dinner was usually half a bagel, dry salad leaves, and a green apple: my mother let me eat in my bedroom; my father, on the weekends I was with him, too.

I have no memory of what I answered, but I know it wasn't satisfactory, because I left with the pit in my stomach heavier than before. I know that Principal H. didn't ask me about the changes in my social life, because I kind of wished she had. I do know that she told me that the eighth-grade dress code forbade any shoes with heels.

And that was it. The only time that I was ever confronted about my burgeoning anorexia. No one tried to stop me, not my parents, not my friends; no other teacher ever sat me down. In my K-12 girls' school, anorexia was a condition draped in sophistication and mystique. Just as we knew which girls were already on their periods, or the ones who had French-kissed, we suspected the bulimics and we knew who watched their calories, but we didn't confront our classmates about their changing bodies: we gossiped, we observed. One of the girls we'd gone through middle school with went anorexic as a freshman: behind her back, the athletes called her "Cucumber" because she ate only four cucumber slices for lunch. For years.

Though the girls who were "weird about eating" were not looked up to in our school, they nevertheless represented a choice that we could make at any time—sphinxes we could succumb to or circumvent on the journey to adulthood. I remember hallway gossip about an older beauty, a junior at that time, who had apparently had anal sex with a basketball star while on cocaine and bled because of her bulimia, a rumor none of us questioned, but instead absorbed as proof that this girl operated in a different orbit. We didn't think her fragile, we thought her aloof and untouchable, code words, I think, for cool. This girl changed schools—we assumed it was because of the varsity-level sex we'd all heard about—and when I saw her a year later in a drivers' ed class, she had bloomed to two hundred pounds from the double digits she'd been at our high school. It scared me, that sudden weight gain, her smiling, swollen face. I was embarrassed for her. I said hello back, but that was it, the extent of our interaction during those days I learned to drive. I am ashamed of this, also: all the opportunities I missed to reach out to other people when—and while—I wanted so badly to be seen and held myself.

6

TROPHY WIFE

"There are so many *horses*," Leo says as we aim our boxy car up North Street, the road that runs through rural Greenwich like a dark pregnancy line. It is the summer of 2005 and we are engaged to be married: fresh off the airplane from the France I have lived in since graduating college, the country Leo has resided in since birth.

I hadn't prepared Leo for the Greenwich of my childhood: the gated driveways and the six-car garages, the fleet of brown landscapers weed whacking and lawn mowing and hedge trimming the properties of white homeowners into an illusion of control. Though the 06830 zip code stands for money in New England, the proximity of my hometown to New York City was the only thing that interested the French. For the six years that I lived in Paris working as a French-to-English translator by day and—incongruently—a party promoter by night, I didn't talk about my childhood; I was barely asked.

This obfuscation suited me, as I wasn't what I had been. Physically, I was transformed: the dark brown hair I'd grown up under was now heavily highlighted, blond enough that my husband-to-be's friends called me "Britney Spears." After fourteen years of wearing a school uniform, it had taken me some time to find my style, sartorially, but I'd found it thanks to the thrift stores and consignment shops that revealed themselves in the twists and turns of my new city: tea-length skirts, eccentric blouses, round-toe shoes with kitten heels, and a fair amount of neon. I never left the house without my statement electric-blue eyeliner smudged under both eyes.

And I'd saved my body. In college, I'd fallen in love with a card-carrying hedonist who wasn't having it with my carefulness around food. Rami was the kind of guy who ordered two appetizers at restaurants when he couldn't choose between them, who took dessert to go because if you didn't want dessert then, you'd surely want it later—a man who came from a family that was sautéing, frying, or boiling something even in the wee hours of the night. Rami's associations between love and food were buttressed by the fact that eating was a highly social experience back in college. Getting together to eat was what my college friends *did.* There were no proper mealtimes: there was meeting-up-for-coffee time, after-dinner cookies from the Meeting Street Cafe in Providence that were the size of a frisbee, "fro-yo" at the snack bar when the college library closed at night, scrambled eggs and fried potatoes at Louis Family Restaurant after a late night out. To not participate in these get-togethers was to miss out on social bonding, but to show up and not share food was even worse. I started joining my friends in their late-night pig-outs, and—although the first time I ate french fries it felt like my body was going to quadruple in size right there at the diner booth—I continued eating the soft-serve yogurt and the lo mein and the endless bowls of cereal available at the university cafeteria. And once I saw that my body did not, in fact, quadruple in size overnight, I ate a little more.

Looking at photos of myself in college now, I can see the weight I put on, a few pounds more than the freshman fifteen. I didn't feel bad about my changing body when I was in college, nor do I now. I was happy. The current me is happy that I let myself get happy.

But now I'm back in my Connecticut hometown, a place where I'd had problems, had felt angry and alone. I'd imagined the presentation of my Greenwich life to Leo as a rococo showcase: the life-sized chess pieces on the grass checkerboard outside my father's library that were too heavy and cumbersome to move; the flashy neighbors with their face-lifts and omnipresent sunglasses; the legendary parties where hostesses rented giraffes and peacocks to hammer home a theme or flooded their own living rooms so the younger guests could skate.

It was overboard and gauche, some of the things that I'd grown up around, but there was love behind the excess, and it was still my life. I wanted to communicate this to Leo, that yes, he was going to see a lot of funny things during our visit, but he couldn't make too much fun.

I glanced out the window at the horse pastures that Leo had mentioned earlier, the black fencing that was the rage back then, the thoroughbreds dressed in fly masks and fly sheets to look like armored knights. "I used to be a horse girl," I offered, failingly. "I used to ride."

Leo looked askance at me. This was something I hadn't mentioned, a former love he'd never met. My mother, who moved homes post-divorce with the addiction of the restless, had asked my permission to throw out all my trophies and my show ribbons when I was in college, and had. I never so much as saw a horse my six years in France, never spoke of equines. My passion for horses had been replaced with writing, a thrill that was now complemented by love and easy happiness with a solid and good man.

"I used to jump," I said. "I had a pony. I used to ride all the time."

His eyes widened. "You had a *horse?*"

I felt pride at the fact that I hadn't come off—to my own fiancé—as the type of person who had had a pony as a child. Entitlement was a fragrance I wanted bleached off my skin. Though I grew up wealthy, I realized from an early age that none of what my father provided was actually mine, and that the only way to be deserving of money was to make money yourself. I have my father to thank for that epiphany—he refused to give me an allowance. After the divorce, my mother would slip me money for pizza and bake sales, but at thirteen years of age, when "sushi" entered the list of things that my friends used daddy's credit card to cover, I took matters into my own hands and applied for the first of many retail jobs: salesgirl at a vintage costume shop, bookseller in the "arts and crafts" section at Borders, barista at Starbucks, crepe maker, deli girl. When I did join my girlfriends on those sushi outings, I ordered steamed carrots and a side of unbuttered rice, cloaking my eating disorder under the mantle of poor pay. My friends treated me like an oddball, but I was outsizedly proud of my side jobs. It mattered less to me that I was going to Saturday-night parties with Frappuccino in my neck creases than that I had a bank account and what I was putting into it was money I had earned.

When I met Leo, I was living in an arrondissement four neighborhoods north of the chic section of Paris, working in alcohol distribution for a company that equipped me with blow-up bottles of beer for late-night Corona Extra parties. My last boyfriend had been a graffiti artist who lived in a defunct elementary school that had neither heat nor water. It was true that I was very far from the horse pastures and private schools I'd known as a girl.

But the big houses flanking the arrival of my own belied that bohemian posturing. It wasn't that Leo had never fraternized with wealth—for a brief period in his childhood, his raincoat-salesman-turned-art-dealer father made some savvy deals and lived large—it was more that "rich" looked so much different in America than it did in France. From the way that people shopped for food (meal by meal in France, versus stockpiling supplies via wholesale clubs in America) to the size of their houses (French 1-percenters were more likely to put surplus income into the upkeep of one discreet vacation home versus the financing of a mushroom network of McMansions), wealth in the US was loud and garish. In France, it was quiet.

Greenwich wasn't quiet. As we drove through the flashy stonework of the gated development my father lived in, Leo's eyes grew wide. I put the car in neutral in front of an actual metal barrier, and a man came to our car with a clipboard to inquire who we were—it had been more than a year since my last visit, the guard was someone new. By the time we rolled past the twelve-bathroom faux-European manors to the serpentine driveway of my dad's own home, where not one but three Saint Bernards romped around in a show of big-breed health, Leo was laughing out loud at the absurdity before him. An American flag flapped from a newly installed flagpole. Two Bernese mountain dogs came out to join the Saint Bernards. My blond stepmother waved from the front porch where she was rolling alternating stripes of white and black paint onto the deck in preparation for our approaching nuptials, which we would celebrate at my father's house.

I'm glad that we milked the proximity of my parents for all the comfort it was worth when we were carving out a new life in the United States. My mother, on her fifth home then, was living in a nice place near Candlewood Lake in New Milford; my Dad on home two in Greenwich. Over the course of the year and a half that Leo and I would try to make it as struggling artists in Brooklyn, I was grateful for the leftovers that were always in my parents' refrigerators should we appear, the washing machine at my mother's that ran better than the one at my father's because of all the dog hair, the rain forest showerhead in my stepmother's bathroom that made me feel like I was Daryl Hannah in *Splash*, turning back into mermaid form. At the point of Leo's visit, I'd been in Connecticut three months to his one: I'd come over early to sort out details for our wedding and start searching for an apartment. Though I would lose comped access to my father's country club in September when I turned twenty-six, I'd been enjoying the hell out of that perk through June and hot July, rinsing off the indignity of manuscript rejection letters in a swimming pool on someone else's dime.

So I guess it was my gratitude for those summer swims that encouraged my father and stepmother to sit us down that day with glasses of champagne (a nectar never opened in my strictly red wine house) to present us with our wedding gift: a membership to their country club. It would be such a fun reward and a relief for us, my father pledged, an oasis from the concrete jungle of our new lives in New York. My stepmother, especially, saw the club as a stepping-stone to the futures we would form: the club was a place where we could put our future children in day camp, the golf course would be ground zero for my non-golfing husband to network with investors for his future films.

This lavish gift was shocking. Not only was my father notoriously thrifty with special-occasion presents, but Leo and I were already having doubts about our New York transition, which I was certain I'd expressed. At one month in to the Brooklyn all the trend pieces had been raving about, it already felt like we were trying to stick a three-pronged European plug into a two-pronged outlet. At twenty-six and twenty-seven, respectively, we were marrying young compared to the people in our circle, and this, combined with our preference for dinner parties over bar hopping, made us feel out of touch and old. Leo's English was pretty terrible at that point, and he didn't understand my fast-talking friends' clubby, pop-culture references. Four weeks in a poorly ventilated apartment, freelancing as box openers for magazine prop stylists, was enough to get us thinking that if we had to pay fourteen hundred dollars to live across from a clogged highway, we might as well go somewhere where we could have trees.

I know I'd expressed our temptation to "go country" to my parents because they'd already put us in touch with a friend of theirs who knew the Adirondacks well, a region we were dreamily scouring fixer-uppers in, online, when we weren't dusting off miniature dutch ovens for *Food & Wine* magazine shoots. And while my parents knew that I intended to "make it" as a writer, and Leo as a filmmaker, I'm not sure if they thought this "making it" would happen on the side of having corporate jobs or what, because they seemed convinced that whatever direction I pointed our life's ship at, polo shirts and tee times and active portfolio management would safely steer us to it. The truth was that I had felt like a mammal in a fish tank for so long, I had to go all the way to Europe to find someone who agreed. While I loved everything my father gave me as a child, I did not want to graft my own marriage—or career—onto what my father built.

As my parents waited on our answer, I clutched both the champagne flute and the smile on my face, trying to discern where the catch was hiding. Cunning and a little mischievous, my father didn't put a turkey on the Thanksgiving table unless he'd won the bird in a tournament of some kind. Although he loved me, he could be underhanded in the ways he showed me that. On my sixteenth birthday, he drove me to the home of a man who walked a black pig out on a porch and handed me the leash. "This is your birthday present," my father said, indicating the pig. That was another gift that I refused, a gift that my father, years later, admitted to hoping I'd accept so that it would cause a ruckus for my mother, who had custody of me then.

I felt closer to my fiancé upon leaving Greenwich on that visit than I had on the drive there. We'd arrived with a conviction; we left with a choice. Perhaps my father and stepmother didn't see the life I'd chosen as appropriate, but if I course-corrected to the right path, I'd get a country club membership and I could be part of a family that shared a universal language and a chit account. Or maybe it really was as simple as my father winning a free membership and wanting to pass that bounty on to us. In any case, it didn't matter—I knew my father well enough to understand that the club membership was a once-in-a-lifetime offer, that we couldn't, for example, ask for the value of the membership in cash instead, but I also knew myself by then, and I knew my almost husband: we turned the membership down.

As we drove out of the manned gate that shielded the Conyers Farm community from its gated counterparts, I told Leo about the man who'd built the residential development and his supermodel wife. The wife in question was Stephanie Seymour, the hell-raiser of Guns N' Roses fame, and her husband was a magazine magnate, a polo player, and a big collector of art. "He has a life-sized, naked bust of his wife hanging in his office," I said. "Like the figureheads on boats." I leaned forward and cupped my breasts in my own hands, looking fish-eyed out the windshield while Leo drove us back to Brooklyn. "It was made by Maurizio Cattelan," I added, a bad-boy artist we admired for his taxidermy offenses against the pope. The sculpture was originally called *Stephanie*, but it came to be called *Trophy Wife* when it was put up for auction during the couple's wayward divorce proceedings. "The husband commissioned it. Don't you think that's nuts?"

But Leo had found so much of that Greenwich visit crazy, the fact that our neighbor had half of his wife's body jutting out of a wall didn't move him north or south. He had other questions, like whether my father actually liked dogs. And why did Americans have so many refrigerators? Why did all the houses fly the flag?

We drove back to our overheated highway apartment astonished by the fact that we found the same things funny, astonished by our easy affinity, astonished by the way you could build a new life out of air and shared desires on the foundation of young love.

I didn't want children—I was mouthy enough about that that my mother had taken to introducing me to people as the daughter who didn't want her to have grandchildren—because children would take away my freedom and my determination to make art. I assumed—because we never talked about it—that a childless, art-filled life was what Leo wanted too.

What a feeling that was, being in touching distance of everything I yearned for. I had a book manuscript in the making and an almost-husband who liked overeating pasta as much as I did, a man who considered a bottle and a half of Fat Bastard wine and two hours of *House Hunters* a stellar Friday night. A year and a half after that particular visit to my parents', we would close on a dilapidated log cabin in the Massachusetts Berkshires that even the real estate agent begged us not to purchase, a place we were so charmed by that our real estate lawyer drove forty-five minutes out to understand why we wanted to possess a place that lacked a functioning septic system and had a foundation filled with holes.

The house was a red log cabin on a dirt road perched over a river with a true blue swimming hole that I would lower myself into eight years later when I was hot and pregnant. It had a random outbuilding that would be just right for Leo's editing equipment, and we could project movies against the building's walls. It had a family of foxes underneath what might have been called a back porch if it hadn't rotted, and a garden planted with the former owner's neckties and discarded roofing tiles. It was a mess, 10 Tannery Road was, but it was our mess: it was intoxicating and endless, the freedom that I felt then to redefine the word "home."

7

BLUE HORS MATINÉ

I park the Nissan Cube we've replaced our totaled Toyota with outside what appears to be a covered riding arena. It's the first time I've come anywhere near an equestrian facility in over thirty years. The dirt gives way under my car tires: it's been a rainy fall.

I'm not at this barn in northern Massachusetts to ride—or so I tell myself. I am here to *research*. With the September 2015 deadline for my second novel missed, I'm trying to play catch-up. There is a male character in my manuscript who is a dressage champion with a horse-breeder mother who works out of a barn near the ocean in Cape Cod. I know precious little about either of these undertakings, and so I've driven two hours north from the Berkshires to talk to someone who does: Amanda Traber, a famed dressage trainer whose barn is near the Cape but not on it, because one of the first things Amanda will set straight about my fiction is that it costs an unholy fortune to have a horse barn by the sea.

To quiet the sheepishness I feel about imposing my quest for fleshed-out characters onto a busy stranger, I run through the questions I've prepared. What makes a dressage horse talented? How did Amanda get into the sport? How does she talk about her passion to people who don't ride? I feel both ill at ease and excited to be at a stable as a writer instead of as a rider. It steadies my nerves to focus on the writing part.

Amanda is waiting for me just past the stall mats in the facility's entrance, and the short walk gives me several beats to collect myself after the smash of the barn smell. Once I actually start riding again, I will talk with women who were pulled back into horse madness by the siren of that smell alone.

In terms of the perfume hitting, there is the animal musk first—the sun-warmed, dirty honey of the place where large head meets muscled neck, the encapsulated summer scent of flaked hay, peaty manure, the reek of riding gloves that never truly dry, the stench of humid fly sheets folded by horse stalls. But underneath these organic smells lie the deeply personal: the acrid punch of the oil dripping underneath my mother's waiting Wagoneer, the sudden tang of cologne wafting up from the front hall, which meant my father was home from Wall Street early. The smell of the linseed oil my mother rubbed and rubbed on my giant Christmas present in hopes that the wooden horse would be easier to rock.

"Remind me what you need again?" Amanda asks. "Did you want to ride?"

Taking in Amanda's assertive stance, the way she stands balanced but also ready to pounce, I recall the knotted energy of the trainers I knew when I was little. She has no time to waste and she doesn't know me beyond my introductory email: I am taking time.

I remind her that I'm an author—I've brought her my first novel. I'm currently working on a book that has a dressage rider in it, and I don't know much about the sport. Amanda blinks at my babbling. Okay, yes, I don't know anything at all.

"But did you ever ride?"

I wave my hand through the air—I rode, it's been forever, it's been thirty years. I don't tell her that this is my first time back in a barn—in any barn—or that the way the girl to the right is cupping her horse's hoof to clean it makes my stomach tight with envy.

I follow Amanda to her office, which doubles as the viewing room nobody uses to watch lessons because the Plexiglas windows are always coated with dust from the arena. Horse blankets of varying weights and stocky bags of grain cover seat and floor. Amanda's desk has a half inch of debris on it: dust, dirt, horsehair. She sits on her desk's edge; I sit on feed bags. I tell myself that I can do this: I can interview someone about what it is like to ride a horse without getting back on one myself. Because I know—I know—if I get on a horse, it will open the floodgates to something that would take a lot of free time and disposable income to retrieve.

When I return to my car after our interview, my chest is hot and tight. I put my notebook and my stupid notes on the seat beside me. Half of my brain is proud that I am doing the writer thing, that I'm being professional, that I drove two hours out here because I want to make my characters feel as real as possible. The other half of me feels like a voyeur, like someone staring through the window at something I can't admit I want. What the hell are this dressage dude and his racehorse-breeding mother doing in my novel about techie consumerism? My agent keeps on telling me that she loves these characters, but I'm forcing square pegs into round holes: they have no place in this book. Deep inside my stomach where I know why my book keeps failing, I also know she's right.

I drive out of the riding facility until I find a gas station. Once there, I find the glummest corner, kill the engine, and let go of the tears that I've been holding back. When I've settled, I rewatch the video that is the reason I've let a fictional dressage rider take up so much room in the first place: a poorly filmed clip of the Danish rider Andreas Helgstrand and his famed mount, Blue Hors Matiné, performing a hallucinatory horse dance in a darkened ring to Tina Turner's "The Best."

Though I came upon this video when Nina was still an infant, revisiting it brings me back to where I was the first time that I saw it: overtired, all milked out, my postpartum hormones like Eurorail trippers in a comedown after a three-day rave. I'd been trying for months to breastfeed my daughter, but there just wasn't enough milk, and my husband, without making much ado about it, had mixed her a bottle of formula, which she'd greedily slurped down. I was feeling like a failure even though I didn't particularly like breastfeeding, was not a nouveau homesteader like some mothers in my region who breastfed into their children's threes and fours. But still, I wanted to be sensual and connected to my child, I wanted to be a fount, you know, of softness and fertility, and the fact that I couldn't produce enough sustenance for my baby left me feeling frigid and carved out. Leo was putting Nina down for a nap, and I was in our second-story bedroom staring out at the backyard. My computer was in front of me, and as so many of us do now in the information age, I reached for that computer to show me something that would make me feel less sad.

I don't remember what I typed, but I know I asked for something beautiful. Show me something beautiful. The most beautiful video in the world. Even though I hadn't looked at a horse on purpose since I'd been a child, some pernicious algorithm offered up the shaky video of Helgstrand and his horse, a whitish-gray one, like all of the horses that had first intoxicated me.

I didn't know anything about dressage then, but I knew that it was hard. It's challenging enough to get a horse to walk in a perfect circle, let alone canter in one with its head down, its knees punching the same invisible air point each time. The amphitheater was small but packed, like a country rodeo but in Denmark, with Eurovision music and Eurovision strobes.

There was an overhead projection of the couple playing before Blue Hors and her rider actually came out, accompanied by whoops and thunderous clapping that could spook a lesser horse. Then the spotlights tightened: one white and one red, and the pair danced out to the strains of Tina Turner. There was an opening here for laughter—the whole thing was pretty cheesy—until the camera zoomed in on the horse's willing expression: her mouth gentle, her eyes soft, her massive head tucked into a frame, and her hooves pointed delicately, but also with such force. Her ears bobbed back and forth in concentration and her tail gracefully switched as she moved her rider across the sand arena to befitting lyrics: this horse was simply the best.

I started to cry watching that video, hard enough that I had to close my bedroom door. It wasn't just the beauty and determination of the lovely horse beneath the rider, it was the fact that these two were so obviously and completely a team, out there in their own world, bonded in a harmony that was probably hard-won.

They were in a world apart, a land of micro-movements and repetitions and foam around the bit, a land whose native language I was rusty in, but spoke. I was watching love.

I scrolled through the many comments to see if other people had had as strong a reaction to the video as I had, and learned the horse was dead. Blue Hors had been a prizewinner, a showstopper of an animal, this champion rider's favorite steed, and she had had a stupid, simple nothing of an accident in a pasture that left her with a broken leg that couldn't be repaired.

My husband called up the stairs to me—there was something in our bedroom that he needed for Nina's nap, and I was pulled away from the film clip, but I thought of it for days; I watched it over and over. I kept thinking about what it would be like for Helgstrand to perform on another horse, to know that he would never have an animal companion who would move under him like Blue Hors, the extent to which the special relationship he'd had with that mount kept him from (or aided him in?) the development of his relationships with humans.

It is such a special union, a mounted human and a horse. It is precarious and dangerous and full and so unique. Watching that video in my new car after what felt like a bogus interview, I cried because I wanted it. I wanted it again.

8

HORSE IN HAND

I'm not alone in being horse-mad; history is too. Horses have been around—and been useful—for so long that there's an argument to be made that it was horses, not dogs, who were humans' first best friend.

Primitive equids were so integral to the history of personhood that paleontologists call them "dawn horses"—there from the beginning. As their habitat changed from jungle to grassland, the equids' heads elongated and their eye sockets moved apart laterally so they could graze while looking out for predators. The dawn horses were watching the stooped anthropoids that would become us, and we were watching them.

Historically, horses have been used for: battle, stature, tilling, transport, breeding, consumption, polo, steeplechasing, hunting, betting, herding, roping, vaulting, barrel racing, jousting, dressage, show jumping, horseball, and a myriad of other disciplines and pastimes. For centuries, horses have been both companion and resource, a ruler that our time on earth can be measured against, proof that we humans can victor, overcome.

Rare are those who—having no experience with horses or with riding—decide that horse contact is what they need to boost their mental health. But horse professionals know the healing a certain kind of person can find within a horse. "They can cleanse you in a manner," says Mark Stalks One, a caretaker of Native horses at the Sacred Way Sanctuary in Florence, Alabama, in a video about the unique creatures he oversees. "They can pull that heaviness from you. . . If someone has an opportunity to find that connection with this wonderful creation, this pony, I say, yes. Without a doubt."

I was at a birthday party for a three-year-old when I met a man—aloof and polyglamorous—who apologized that he couldn't kiss me hello in greeting because he'd "just come from the barn." This comment struck a chord in me: Someone in my age range was a rider? I spent the next twenty minutes wincing as our children whacked at a piñata, trying not to ask this man about his barn.

Because that would be dangerous. Though I didn't know what riding cost when I was little because my Wall Street father paid for it, it certainly *looked* like it cost a lot. Glossy Range Rovers and Barbour jackets and Burberry scarves, horses too expensive to be put in a paddock, fly masks and horse blankets of seven different weights, the clothing needed to get on a horse, the gear needed to ride, all of it—the *all* of it—was so far outside the range of what I was making as a freelance writer that it would be the height of ir-responsibility even to ask the name of this man's stable.

But as I sat there urging my daughter to eat the birthday cake whose raspberry coulis violated her anti-red-food stance, tallying up the candy wrappers I would help the hostess gather from the piñata-speckled floor, I felt a protest rise. I needed something for myself. Something that had nothing to do with sisterhood or motherhood or being a good spouse. Something that would make up for the fact that when the couples therapist we'd hired to help us out of the mire asked if there had been infidelity in our marriage, Leo answered, "No," and I had to raise my hand—I actually raised my hand—to contradict him: "Yes."

"But that didn't count," he said. I stared at him, and then I stared at our marriage counselor, who had an office full of prayer flags. Didn't count because I hadn't let my transgression develop into something that we couldn't have returned from, or didn't count because Leo hadn't been attached enough to me to care?

I cared. I was counting.

I had too many identities and very little me. I walked past the fallen candy on the carpet and asked the man for the number of the person who'd taught him how to ride.

•

Horsemen and women have been noting the transformational potential of human and equine interaction far earlier than 1969, when the official body that governs equine therapy in America was formed. In 300 BC, the Greek physician Hippocrates wrote that "riding in clean air strengthens body muscles and keeps them in good form," a sentiment that would be echoed thousands of years later by the British statesman Lord Palmerston (but credited to Winston S. Churchill on a legion of fridge magnets): "There's something about the outside of a horse that is good for the inside of a man."

That horseback riding is good for the repairing and strengthening of a person's muscles is indisputable to most who try it, but the uninitiated are slower to recognize how a horse can help the mind. Frequently referred to as a "stealth therapy," interaction with horses has been known to benefit people who struggle with anxiety, depression, post-traumatic stress, and fearfulness, because horses mirror human emotions. If you aren't calm, the horse won't be, either, and denial doesn't get you far with a herd animal. You can spin an interaction with another human any dozen ways, but when you're with a horse, you can read how your relationship is going in real time. Their ears are forward, neutral, or pinned back: they're attentive, relaxed, on guard. You know, quite literally, where you stand with a horse, and this candidness has proved beneficial to people with certain emotional and/or physical impediments.

But on my drive out to the White Bridge riding facility in Litchfield for my comeback lesson, I wasn't thinking about my mental health. I was allowing a victory film to play out in my head: me walking up a barn aisle to confront a steed only I could understand. We would wow them in the arena ("No one else can ride him!"), and the instructor would pull me aside after, desperate to help me realize my potential ("Where in the world have you *been*?").

Which is to say that even though it had been three decades since I'd been on a horse, I assumed I still possessed a talent for it, or at the very least, a knack. One of the many reasons I'd been hesitant to schedule a lesson was that I thought I'd be turbo-boosted back to the level I'd been at when I stopped: if my first lesson was on a Wednesday, inconvenient though it was for my family, I'd be jumping in horse shows again by Saturday.

Which is why life, the greatest comedian, presented me with a German instructor who was safety first and second, and who considered "fun" something to be had with horses after you'd been riding fifty years. Katja wasted no time in telling me that I would be riding on a longe line—a nylon rope wound through the horse's bridle that would allow her to manipulate the horse's movements while I sat astride him. I was mortified by this announcement— would it even count as riding?—and then Katja presented me with a walkie-talkie and a convoluted earpiece that I had to fit under my helmet so I could hear her in the ring.

Okay, I said to my wounded ego, so what if you're on a longe line like a five-year-old? Lean in and take the holy waters of the horse. And there it was: the peat smell of an ending summer, oiled leather, hay wet with rain. The horse was as black as the sharp keys on a piano, with magnificent brown eyes. My heart sang out to this great beast and he answered with a toot through his gigantic nostrils. I was dressed. The horse was tacked. It was time to go.

The indoor arena at White Bridge was was formidable, nearly Olympian in size. Katja and I headed to the unsavory part of the ring—the dark bit by the entrance gate where horses tend to spook—leaving passage for the preteens tearing over jumps made from fake bricks and hay on gleaming mounts. Katja made a final adjustment to the gangly earpiece slipping from my helmet and told me to get up on the mounting block—the mini staircase that you use to spare yourself (and the horse's back) the ungainliness of getting on without one. That three-step block felt like a diving board. There would be a before and an after to this, surely. I stood still in my before.

•

For women in rural areas who are parents or caretakers of small children, the motor vehicle is a confession booth, the red tent, the place where we can exult or break down. I sat in the parking lot for a long time after that first lesson, trying to understand the surge of feelings I was having. I had only walked and trotted, and yet the heat of that beast underneath me, the breadth of his body and the pump of his great heart, had touched something primitive inside. For the first time in months on end, my mind wasn't racing. I didn't want to look at my phone to confirm that other people appeared to be having more success/fun/sex than I was. I didn't want to rush to the next thing on my agenda, I only wanted to sit, and feel, and be.

Later, I would learn about the intelligence of horse hearts: how the massive electromagnetic field around a horse's heart is five times larger than ours and, accordingly, can influence how our own hearts beat. The simple act of approaching a horse can cause a human's heart rate to slow, and the pleasant, easy contact between a horse and a human admirer (scratches on the neck, having a horse puff air out on your face) can stimulate the release of oxytocin, a neurotransmitter known as the "cuddle hormone" associated with positive touch.

Positive, selfless touch was something I was in need of in my thirty-eighth year on earth. The baby who had lived her life strapped to my chest, cooing and blowing bubbles into my exposed skin, was now a toddler who wanted to do everything herself, who squirmed out of my arms when I was craving intimacy, who survived on cheese crackers and apple cider instead of my own milk. My body seemed invisible; it wasn't looked at by my husband, and because we lived in the middle of the woods in an already rural area, it wasn't looked at by anybody else. When I contemplated my own body, I recognized it needed help. The prior year, I'd seen two separate nutritionists for what I'd self-diagnosed as irritable bowel syndrome, but it proved to be something more inscrutable than that: no matter how much I ate or when I ate it, I couldn't keep weight on.

When I scheduled that comeback riding lesson, I was on a battery of supplements and an antidepressant that Joe the therapist had a psychiatrist prescribe. I was taking ashwagandha extract to lower my cortisol, iron for my anemia, probiotics for my gut health, milk thistle for digestion, rehmannia herb and a sleeping pill called Donormyl for insomnia, paroxetine HRI for my depression . . . Lavender oil (for anxiety) was ruining my sheets. While the ritual of swallowing bitter roots each morning made me feel like I was participating in a self-care regimen that would protect me from my darker urges, these pills and oils and extracts didn't work. Sure, they helped a little—extending my ability to be patient with my daughter and my husband by several minutes, definitely—but these supplements were Band-Aids on the kneecap of depression, and the paroxetine got me so jazzed up it made my insomnia worse.

The horse contact, though, that contact reached out with its superpower and breathed into my soul, the chilly place that wished it could be loved differently and learn how to love better. I told Katja I'd love to come again the following Tuesday if she had room for me; we could do one lesson a week. I counted the hours between the lesson that had just concluded and the next time I could ride with the anticipation of somebody at the beginning of a love affair.

9

SIRES AND DAMS

The moon was shining so brightly that I didn't need the light in the stairwell. Nina's cries were sweet more than they were plaintive: 3:00 AM, this was our hour.

I grab my big book off the living room table where I'd left it, fetch a glass of water from the kitchen sink. The nurses at my postnatal checkups told me that the breastfeeding schedule I was on with Nina was untenable: if she kept feeding for an hour every five hours like this, my milk would run out. But I didn't want to give up the peace that we had found. Five-hour naps, and she was just an infant! Five hours in which I could catch up on work and write and anchor myself in my professional identity before lolling back into the yummy haze of early motherhood. What a comfort and a luxury: one hour together in the quiet of predawn, the embrace of the chair that held us perfectly and the faux-fur blanket draped across our bodies, the reading lamp Leo had installed so that I could escape into a story while my daughter fed.

These journeys into the hideaway of mother/daughterhood were even more entrancing since I'd discovered the bobcat. It was

November, and the snow had fallen early. Each morning, round and round the back of our log cabin, we discovered giant cat tracks. Our beloved Maine coon cat had died from heart problems just before Nina's birth, and he was buried in the backyard: this represented the death of an animal whom I'd imagined being a great friend to Nina, almost a de facto sibling. Mylo, as we had called him, had a kind and funny nature and was the size of a raccoon. He'd died early at seven—his breed's life expectancy was fifteen. Because I kept finding cat tracks, and had even spotted the bobcat once in the light of snow and moon, I got it into my head that this large cat held the spirit of my smaller, dead one; that our pet had sent himself to watch over our daughter. Accordingly, those twilight feedings were something of a charging station for my confidence. Whatever tiredness I was feeling, whatever manifestations of disbelief were coursing through me—because wasn't I the one who said that I was never having children?—were forced into retreat by those magical evenings while a big cat pawed the ground. This was the animal connection that no one could put into words, the coming together of a mother and her child in a way that was old enough to feel preordained. I felt powerful during those mergings; beautiful and necessary. It was a privilege on those moon nights to be alive, awake.

In the winter of 2016, we would move out of that log cabin in the Massachusetts Berkshires for a house just across the border in Litchfield County, Connecticut. Though our new town was only twenty-five minutes away from our old one, it came with major upgrades. Not only was there a functioning general store that carried milk and toilet paper, there was also a day care and a public elementary school. Though I was excited for the conveniences our new home would afford, the terror started coming for me just before that move. The year 2015 was a stressful time to be a woman: *Roe v. Wade* was being challenged, pussies were being grabbed, schoolchildren were being gunned down by pimpled white boys who felt that they were entitled to more than what they had. The notion that danger is everywhere is a feeling that most new mothers can attest to the moment they move with their new charge from the birthing bed into a world of drunk drivers and killer bees, but it seemed that there was an awful lot of proof—more proof than there should be—that it would be difficult to keep someone you loved alive that year.

Behind closed doors I was uploading cries for help to my Facebook page: strongly worded posts about gun violence and the need for physical protest. Although I had a fair number of followers, those posts received no likes or comments or check-ins, not even from my husband or relatives, which cemented my suspicion that I was attuned to a frequency that other people couldn't hear. I remember having a coffee one time with a friend at an outdoor table and admitting to her all the terror attached now to my mundane actions: grocery shopping, driving, walking on a driveway scarred with snow and ice.

I don't remember our conversation exactly, but I recall my girlfriend saying that she was under pressure, too, that it was "a lot" to have a young child. *It isn't that,* I wanted to scream, *it isn't about that. We are all in danger!* For the hundredth time that year, I had the sensation that my loved ones were sleepwalking through a nightmare world.

This certainly felt like the case at home, where all I wanted was permission to fall apart, and I wasn't getting it. Before Nina, there had been periods when either my work or Leo's took precedence, but for so long, this imbalance looked only like one of us getting more attention or opportunities than the other. While this occasionally caused feelings of inadequacy or jealousy, it didn't necessitate either of us sacrificing time on our respective craft. With our daughter, though, Leo and I were suddenly forced into a more explicit seesaw situation where one season—or an entire year—had to be about one person, and the next would be about the other, so that if I had a book coming out, and knew that I would be doing publicity and touring around the country, Leo would have both his hands on deck. In a film year for him, when he was immersed in postproduction and promoting the film at festivals, the turn on deck would be mine.

But whose year was it, then? For me, the lines were blurry, and I think for Leo, too. It was a surprise to both of us how much I enjoyed our daughter's infancy, my perfectionism and compulsive habits serving me well during a parenting phase that was all about doing highly specific things at specific times. And we were both surprised by how Leo faltered during the same period: how overwhelmed he became—nearly paralyzed—by Nina's cries, her fits. How often he forgot things: her favorite cotton swaddle in the day care bag, my carefully written grocery lists not taken to the store. Altruistic and patient, I'd expected Leo to be the one who soared through Nina's infancy, but he's never been a comfortable multitasker, and that made parenting a newborn challenging for him. I love to multitask, would even say I thrive on it, and I managed to navigate a busy period where I was learning how to parent while shepherding creative work into the world with no indication that I needed to slow down, until I stopped sleeping, and my body started failing, and I couldn't be the person that everyone depended on anymore, but I didn't know how to say this.

So I didn't say anything, and Leo didn't see it—he literally didn't *see* it. Even before the car accident, it seemed like something was off with Leo's field of vision when we lived in the Berkshires. He developed curious balance issues and had difficulty identifying things that were visible to others. I remember him bumping into objects a lot, hitting his head over and over on the too-low doorjambs of our log cabin and stubbing his toe repeatedly on Nina's heavy high chair. Newly insured, I asked Leo to consult a doctor to see if anything was neurologically awry, but the only diagnosis his checkup yielded was "preoccupation." Leo was on the festival circuit for his first film and in the writing and casting stage for his second, and these efforts were so dominant in his psyche, there wasn't room for anything else.

And this included locating things. "Have you seen my . . ." became Leo's standard greeting to me: Have you seen my blue-and-white socks, have you seen the car keys, do you know where our auto insurance ID cards are, do you have the sticker for the dump. Whenever his "*Est-ce que tu as vu*" burned through our cabin to me, I wanted to scream that I was the lost thing that needed to be found. I was the item hiding in plain sight that Leo couldn't see. Looking back now, I think that Leo must have been going through an existential reckoning of his own, but at the time, I only had room for my resentment: if I was freelancing all the time for an ever-changing salary, remembering where the social security cards were and teaching our daughter to wipe her "zizi" down instead of up, trying to meet my book deadline while texting images of the grocery list that Leo had forgotten, performing the various requirements of a sibling/child/parent/spouse/friend/citizen, then there simply wasn't time in the calendar for me to fall apart.

When horses sleep, there is a horse elected as the one who will stay up. Because equines are prey animals, this arrangement is hardwired into them as a survival mechanism: while several horses are getting shut-eye, one horse stays alert at the outside of the herd. Should danger come, he will be ready to neigh them all awake. I'd always wondered if I'd ever find a warning horse for me, a bedmate who would make me feel safe enough to sleep soundly, steadfast in my conviction that he would let me know if danger called. But I hadn't arranged my life that way—I was so certain that people would fail me if I let myself be vulnerable, I never let them try to help, and in shunning potential help for decades, I'd never learned to ask for it. Oddly enough, horseback riding was giving me that language, and what I was learning to say was that I needed an escape room from caretaking. Horses were that place.

·

We have Freud to thank (or curse) for the fallacy that women love to ride because it assuages their alleged penis envy, but a quick look at the wrath rained down upon "horse girls" in online forums suggests that the pushback against women and horses has nothing to do with phallic longing and everything to do with horses giving women independence, freedom, and no small amount of joy. Which is to say that horseback riding makes women hard to control.

History supports this reading; mythology, too. There is a Pawnee Indian tale called "The Woman Who Became a Horse" where a woman so prefers horse companionship to the domestic drudgery waiting for her at home that she transforms partly into a mare. Unable to gallop as fast as a real horse, she is lassoed by her husband when she tries to run away from him, but once home, he's so exasperated by her whinnying that he sets her free and she assumes her destined form. This story takes a darker turn in the legend of the Greek goddess Demeter, who takes the form of a horse and hides in a herd of other horses to escape Poseidon and mourn her beloved daughter, who has recently been abducted by the god of the underworld. Poseidon, little thrilled that the object of his affection is both metamorphosed and grieving, changes himself into a stallion and rapes Demeter as a mare.

Horseback riding offered an escape from my domestic life, a lucky, calm life that both sustained and stifled me. The biscuit smell of my daughter's neck, the dimples in her fingers, the diligent thud of my husband splitting fat logs into firewood lived alongside unwanted tabs on my behavior and my time, clogged the space that used to be filled by adventure with "Soup-er Bowl" school flyers. Curiously enough, though, my horse outlet was helping me to be more successful in my private life.

"I do not think you are breathing?" Katja noted at our second lesson, squinting as if she were reading an eye chart. "You are not breathing, yes? Next time, you come in tighter clothing. So I can see you breathe."

Once she'd called my attention to it, I realized she was right. Not only was I holding my breath around the ring, I wasn't breathing well at home. Blocked breath during the sock wars that I waged with my daughter. Blocked breath while I tried to gauge whether Leo was near the end of a phone conversation or whether some producer would see him default on his promise to help with dinner again. I held my breath until whatever thing I'd bogey-monstered into being had occurred, and the fact that I wasn't breathing usually made the worst-case scenarios come to pass.

This was so embarrassing. What healthy person struggles with inhaling and exhaling? But I had to work to relearn how to breathe; counting an appropriate number of seconds in between my inhale and exhale, making sure that I was letting breath out when I felt anxious. Not only was I making the horse nervous during my lessons ("Why isn't she breathing? Should I stop breathing too?"), but I was doubling my own stress by living on an inhale.

I fished through the shapeless things I'd been wearing to find clothing that would allow Katja to watch my diaphragm rise and fall. I Googled riding videos that celebrated breathing and these videos hypnotized me, setting my brain down into a hammock of oxytocin calm. Something incredible was happening in my home life now that I was focusing on my breath and body, had barns back in my life. I began sleeping through the night for the first time in more months than I could count. I was experiencing . . . patience. The act of walking past a stabled horse and watching its ears flatten because of the stress that I was carrying made me so much more aware of the energy I bore. By the time of that second lesson, I had half a year of therapy behind me and was still seeing Joe once a month. Having someone listen to me in therapy helped me understand how to listen to other people instead of talking over them. Though I still had the panic—I was envisioning accidents and disasters when I allowed my mind to wander—these terrors weren't at the corner of every second of my day. When I felt impatient (which was often now, instead of always), I imagined the obstacle in front of me as a horse whose energy could be influenced by mine. I started breathing differently while I waited for my daughter to coax her socks and shoes on, and found that she did both a whole lot quicker if I wasn't demanding that she hurry, hurry, hurry. When I heard the "*Bonne nuit, mon chat*" that meant Leo had tucked Nina in and was bidding her good night, I let out a big breath instead of holding on to whatever thing I'd wanted to explode to him about after he'd gotten Nina down.

"Thank you," I said, meeting his surprised eyes when he emerged out of her bedroom. I watched his shoulders release tension—we wouldn't fight that night.

I indicated the glass of wine I'd topped up for him, perched precariously on a little wooden bench that we'd been meaning to replace with a proper coffee table for years.

"Tell me," I said. "Tell me how things are going with your film."

I exhaled. So did he. And we started talking. Because I wasn't (literally) holding my breath all the time, it became easier to hear Leo's struggles without being on the defensive. Leo was trying to launch a second feature film with a rap star in the lead role, and he couldn't afford the production support to outsource his many tasks. As he walked me through the circuitous conversations he was suffering with Hollywood agents we called "the taco guys" because they always ended "convos" with the demand that Leo call them if he was in LA so they could go out for tacos, I remembered that this wasn't a pipe dream; this messy, halting, infuriating, seemingly senseless process was how a film got made. I had to be kinder. I had to be more supportive of Leo's second project. And because his flow of freelance editing work from a local skincare client had been dwindling for some time, I had to find a way to stretch our single salary into two. Which meant overriding a desire I'd been having for a second kid.

"A second child for the girl who never wanted a first one," Leo laughed, the first time that I mentioned my stirrings for another baby. When I didn't laugh back, or even smile, he saw that I was serious.

"But we can't have a second kid, you're not even sleeping," he said, his face suddenly tight. "You're not even managing with Nina."

My face went tight too. "Well, maybe if I didn't have to *do* everything," I said, and the match was lit to fight.

In our calmer moments, I was able to hear what he was saying and I knew that it made sense. I wasn't healthy; I wasn't strong. A newborn meant less sleep, not more. And yet, I wasn't getting any younger. If we were going to try for a second kid, that time was now.

But the riding—and the breathing—diluted that sense of urgency. I could see the forest for the trees again. How in the world would I—would we—cope with a second child? How could our marriage bear the strain? It wasn't a second kid I needed, it was a passion, something to sink my time and dreams in. And in horses, I had found it.

"I don't think I need a second child," I wrote in my diary of my secret change of heart. "I just need some new joy." I was feeling hope—the great big coursing "yes" of it—for the first time in so long.

After four lessons with my new instructor, I was feeling something else: the unmistakable landsickness of a new pregnancy.

10

DOUBLE TROUBLE

I was in my bedroom in our South Carolina house with my best friend, Kristin, making up songs on my electronic keyboard as the palm trees began to toss in the overture to yet another storm. It was spring break, and a busy week for us: Kristin and I had decided to shutter the haircutting business we'd started a few days earlier after the only person who responded to the flyers we'd stuffed into the neighborhood mailboxes was my little brother, Brendan, who had not so much agreed to let us work our magic on him as acquiesced. So we were revisiting songwriting as a fast track to creative success, something we had tasted earlier that year when our fellow fifth graders performed one of our lyrical compositions at a Friday middle school assembly. Kristin had a beautiful voice and was a better piano player than I was, so my function in our duo was as the lyricist. We were just hitting our stride when a scream came up from the yard below us. We ran out onto the balcony that hung off my second-story bedroom. My five-year-old brother was floating facedown in the pool.

What I remember afterward is the reflection of the ambulance lights in the puddles left by the storm that did arrive, and the efforts of the first responders to revive my brother via CPR on the wet flagstones around the pool. I don't remember going to the hospital—this wasn't the first time my brother had suffered a sudden seizure, so it had already been established that my role during these crises was to stay home and keep calm. Kristin and I never finished writing the song that we'd been working on. The vacation ended early.

At five years old to my ten, with our parents recently divorced, my brother was transitioning from a willing accomplice to my schemes and fantasies into a vortex of risk and darkness. There was something wrong with him, deeply, deeply wrong with him, and the mystery around his illness was warping our changed family even more. For the past year, Brendan had started to fall unconscious without warning, sometimes going into a seizure that would result in the ambulance coming and the sirens howling and the neighbors pushing aside curtains and coming out onto their lawns to gawk.

The first time it had happened, my parents were still married and I had been at school, and Brendan had fallen unconscious at the top of a staircase leading down into our rec room, tumbling to the very bottom of the stairs, where he was retrieved by our live-in mother's helper, Tony, and my mother, who was also home. This was recounted to me when I returned from school that day—I hadn't been called out of fourth grade to accompany Brendan to the hospital. When I found out what had happened, I felt guilty for having enjoyed pastel painting and a sunny recess while my brother and mother battled something big and real and scary in our home.

My all-girls school had a partner school called Brunswick, but my brother had no chance of going there. Already in kindergarten, Brendan had started showing anger-management issues and cognitive difficulties that worried my mother enough to enroll him in a full psychological evaluation at the Child Study Center at Yale. This study revealed that Brendan was "functioning in the borderline range of cognitive ability," with an IQ of 66. (In 2021, Healthline.com set the average American IQ at 98.) He was enrolled in the Eagle Hill School, a small, private establishment in Greenwich that welcomes children with learning and behavioral challenges, and it was only weeks after his enrollment that he suffered his first seizure—at the time, this was what we called his heart failures because we didn't know what else to name them; these episodes were far more serious than fainting spells, and Brendan seemed too young for the label "heart attack." Months later, Brendan's doctors would rightly identify these incidents as SCDs—sudden cardiac deaths, catalyzed by an electrical problem in the heart. In 1995, only 20 percent of people who suffered a first attack survived. Of these, 80 percent died if they were unlucky enough to have a second episode. Between ages five and seven, my brother suffered—and survived—six sudden cardiac deaths.

These are the topics that are discussed within my family: the weather, dinner preparation, blockbuster movies, how Nina is doing, and the status of Leo's films. Not up for discussion: illness, memories, fear. Anything I know about my father's childhood was given to me like contraband in snippets by my grandmother: photographs and press clippings from local papers about his achievements as a college track and basketball star, very few stories.

81

My own mother is so cagey about her health that in 1996, she pretended to be on a two-week honeymoon in Italy with my step-father when she was actually recovering in a local Connecticut hospital from a stroke she'd had after their wedding because she didn't want to "worry" me.

Given this furtiveness, it isn't surprising that I wasn't en-couraged to ask questions about my brother and his rebel heart. Time wasn't made for questions or reflection, explana-tions or conjecture; actions mattered most. Car rides to Yale New Haven Hospital, phone calls in the middle of the night, ambulances that came frequently enough to our new house on Shore Road that the responders knew our names. We did not *talk* about my brother; we reacted, we performed. Or rather, my mother did. My father, who hadn't been keen on having a second child in the first place, was now the divorced father of a child with extremely complicated and expensive health and behavioral problems, and because my mother proved time and time again that there was nothing she wouldn't do to find out what was wrong with Brendan, his caretaking became my mother's full-time job. In time, it would actually be my step-mother who matched my mother's advocacy for my brother's health, seeding goodwill between them. As for me, I was already drawing on the coping skills of overachievement and perfec-tionism that would both bolster and injure me throughout my adulthood. The worse my brother did in school ("low average intellectual functioning, weak visual and verbal concept forma-tion, inconsistent concentration, impulsivity, and poor visual perceptual skills" were just a handful of the issues that Eagle Hill School's annual cognitive evaluation showed Brendan to have), the more I strived to surpass whatever expectations my own school had set for me.

Academics also provided me with an excuse to talk to my family about what was going on with Brendan. Junior year of high school, my AP history teacher invited his students to do a research paper on any topic we wanted, and I chose my brother's medical history: an undertaking that saw me interviewing key family members as well as my brother's doctors and teachers. My mother let me read Brendan's cognitive and psychological evaluations—access I now realize that I probably shouldn't have been granted—and I remember feeling conflicting emotions as I read over the harsh words in those reports: a kind of relief, because there really was something wrong with Brendan, along with keen defensiveness; these people didn't know my brother, he was sweet, he loved race cars. His bed frame was a wooden race car. It couldn't be this bad.

In middle school and the beginning of high school, my mother had chief custody of me and my brother, and the lesson that I was learning about motherhood during those early years was one of self-erasure and endless sacrifice. "I left you alone a lot," my mother said, when I revisited this episode of our life together on the phone to see if what I remembered about that decade matched up with what she did. "We were always at the hospital. I had a hotel room—we practically lived there." And while my mother's temporary relocation made sense, it's true that I started to identify emotionally as an only child during the years that my brother was hospitalized. Eventually, my mother would become so exasperated with the pressure to parent both my ailing brother and my surging hormones that I moved into my father's house full-time in the middle of high school, which only exacerbated the distance—physical and emotional—between me and my brother.

Before I moved into my father's, though, I was indeed left home alone a lot, but rather than feel bitter or scared about my separation from Brendan, I felt like the chips were falling into place. In order to be a good mom, you had to be a mother like my mother: willing to drop everything at a moment's notice to drive places in an emergency, to stay at a sick person's bedside regardless of what plans you had to cancel and hopes you had to dash. I was not a selfless person, went my teenage thinking; therefore, I could not be a successful, loving mother. By the age of fifteen, I was proudly telling friends and family members that I would never have offspring. Parenting, maternity, none of it was for me.

My family believed me. Why shouldn't they have? When my stepmother and father went on to have one, then two, then three new children of their own, I took as little interest in them as the large dogs that my dad and his new wife were also acquiring: first, the two Bernese mountain dogs, then the three Saint Bernards. Large dogs, large families: it was a life of noise and mess. I wanted a quiet life where the only soundtrack was my thoughts, a life I made easier to come by when I up and left America for France after graduating from college with a degree in comparative literature that would allow me to find work as a translator abroad.

Given that I wasn't equipped with positive associations around siblinghood as a young person, it's indicative of just how blurred my mind was that I thought marital and mental salvation lay in my having a second child. The people most shocked by the fact that I'd had a baby were, in order, my mother, then myself. But I had loved it, loved the everything of early motherhood: my changing body, the shifting of priorities, even the once-in-a-lifetime ravagings of birth. I was at my healthiest and most productive as a pregnant woman. I felt beautiful and vital. After Nina's birth, those positive feelings didn't go away. I was anchored, I felt necessary—as a food source, I was. All I could think of during my lost year was that I wanted all that back: the easy sleep, the focused mind, the permanent anchor. Additionally, I was so petrified about something happening to our daughter, I felt certain that having a second child would make me feel calmer about her lifeline.

"You don't have a second child as life insurance for the first one," Leo would tell me when I angled my second-child argument this way.

"You don't have a second child when you're not even able to really be there for the one you have," was another thing he'd say.

"I don't know if I can love a second child as much as I love Nina," was a courageous third.

Five years was the difference they'd have between them if we gave Nina a sibling. The exact same gap that lay between me and my own brother. My brother, who was cautioned by medical professionals never to have children, who developed a best friendship with our half brothers that survives today; my brother, who loves having a large and discombobulated family and couches covered in dog fur; my brother, who has fine knife skills and likes to make tomato salad drenched in Italian dressing when we get together, which is rarely, less than once a year. My brother, who was the youngest American patient ever to have an automatic implantable cardioverter defibrillator inserted in his stomach to regulate his malfunctioning heart. My brother, who spent his teenage-hood hunched over so that the contours of the box were less visible through his clothing—the AICD unit was large, and he was gruesomely thin. My little brother, who was discovered in 1995 to be the only patient in medical history to possess both a ventricular tachycardia and a ventricular fibrillation, which basically meant that he had two electrical nodes on his heart that were in total conflict with each other, one heart chamber wanting what the other chamber did not.

I had always thought that I was diametrical from Brendan, that our relationship was defined more by our differences than our similarities. But our divided hearts were linked. One side of my heart wanted to try for a second child; the other knew what a risk letting that wish come true would be.

11

PURPLE ISLAND

Lots of people have a story about "the one who got away": a French gynecologist is mine. Dr. Marie-Laure (I loved, first of all, how she went by her first name like a grade-school teacher) practiced out of her home in a contemporary apartment complex in Paris, directly across from France's oldest department store, the upscale Bon Marché.

Regardless of the season, Marie-Laure dressed in an aristocratic style that suited her lithe frame: white denim with gold grommets, a roomy linen blouse of the same shade, supple boat shoes, and the iconic Cartier "Love" bracelet, a gold band with O-shaped locking mechanisms that couldn't be opened without assistance, purportedly that of a lover. If it was winter, Marie-Laure would throw a cashmere sweater around her shoulders and hide—somewhere in the office—her more unsightly street shoes.

Marie-Laure's examination room had wide parquet floor-boards, floor-to-ceiling tinted windows that looked over the Bon Marché's small park, and a shoji screen bent around the

examination table, over which trembled an antique chande-
lier. After the exam, which Marie-Laure would effectuate with
a robin's-egg-blue lab coat over her white outfit, I'd dress behind the screen before joining her at a mahogany partners desk
(a furniture offering that I believe originated in the banking
world, allowing two people to use the same desk while facing
one another). If you can imagine the haughty remove of Bette
Davis inside a French speaker's body, you can envision what
these post-examination downloads with Marie-Laure were like.
Matter-of-fact with no time for mawkishness, her advice regarding my burgeoning femininity was curt, provocative, and
unforgettable.

My first pregnancy found me during a time when I didn't have
health insurance in America, but I was still insured in France.
Because it was the holiday season and we had a trip planned to
visit my husband's family in Paris, I scheduled my first-trimester
screening with my much-missed Marie-Laure. At the end of the
exam, I took my place at the consult desk for what was probably
the last time—it wasn't a sustainable practice, being a pregnant
American with a gynecologist in France—insistent on asking all
the things that an American ob-gyn wouldn't give me straight.

"So I have been wondering," I said, gearing up for my first
question. "Now that my husband and I are back in France and
announcing the pregnancy to everyone, lots of people are offering us champagne. I have this superstition that if you're lucky
enough to be offered it, you should never refuse champagne. Is it
okay to have a little bit?"

"Throughout your pregnancy, try to limit your intake of alcohol to two glasses a day and you'll be fine."

"A day?" I repeated, stunned. Marie-Laure narrowed her eyes at me. If it had been an expression in French, I think she would have asked me if she had stuttered.

My palms were sweating, but I had two remaining questions. "A lot of my friends in America," I began, "they breastfeed until their child is almost two. What is your opinion on breastfeeding?"

Marie-Laure looked at me as if I had offered her cheese before lunch, instead of after.

"Breastfeeding will absolutely ruin your breasts. If you want to demolish them, go right ahead."

It was time for my last question.

"*Docteur*," I said. "I'm interested in natural childbirth. You know, laboring without any medicine. Do you have any thoughts on that?"

Marie-Laure closed her ledger, my check for our appointment functioning as a bookmark.

"That," she said, "is a question for a therapist, not a gynecologist."

•

Marie-Laure would have been incensed by my second pregnancy, not only because I'd let my sentiments drive my desire to get pregnant but also because of the conditions under which the conception took place.

March of 2016 was a damp month that arrived with that most American of traditions: spring break. After a winter cooped up with my insomnia and my shame at not being able to get my second book right, alongside the resentments I was compiling against Leo, my Florida-based mother's assertion that there was nothing she'd like more than some solo time with Nina came as a godsend.

"I'll keep her for a long weekend, and you two go somewhere," my mother offered. "Get some time away."

The valid concern over what in the hell Leo and I would do together, alone, without the buffer of our daughter, lost its power next to the allure of vacation planning, an activity I've always loved. I would identify a place to go, the tech-savvy Leo would rent a car to go there, and we would go—the fact that we weren't speaking to each other or touching could be dealt with once we got there.

Leaving the last-minute lodging details to a chronically under-rested penny pincher was probably an error, because I ended up missing some of the finer print regarding the Florida Keys "Purple Island" rental that I booked.

"Purple Island" was a fitting name for the fetid stilt house just outside Islamorada that I found for our four-night getaway: a one-bedroom (I swear I'd checked "entire house") that turned out to be a rank two-bedroom with a surprise bonus couple in tow. There wasn't a town to walk to, and the nearest beach was more of a latrine where families let their toddlers test out water contact without swim diapers. Our bedroom had a mildew problem that the owner had tried to combat by placing air-purifying crystals all over the place that smelled of Irish Spring. The bonus couple in the bedroom next to ours spent most of their time trying to have sex in the bunk beds that room boasted; in the mornings we made breakfast underneath a laundry line sparkling with the dame's sequined bikinis.

Unsure what to do with our ample adult free time, and eager to get out of the house we were unwittingly sharing with another couple, we walked in the heat past battered conch houses, went to bad art shows. But despite the disappointment around the place I had landed us in, the languid heat of Florida had a healing effect, lengthening my coiled muscles, dimming my sharp thoughts. I was like a frozen stick of butter that had been on the counter for a few minutes: if not softer, softening. What was I so furious about? Why did I hate my mellow husband? Leo had some serious spatial awareness issues (the man would ask me where his shirt was when it was already on his chest) and a selective attention span, but he was a good father and a dedicated one, tireless in fact, and while he'd been toiling for years on the same film project, he also made regular upgrades to our house with the impressive carpentry skills he'd taught himself through video tutorials. Our sensual life had dwindled to once-in-a-blue-moon physical communions that made me feel embarrassed, but when I turned the tables, what desire did I show him? What efforts was I making? How come everything was Leo's fault all the time? My husband had brought this up in the marital counseling sessions we were newly attending—the way my constant disappointments and micromanagements made him feel emasculated, that my seeing the bad in all the good made me an exhausting person to live with. And on top of all this, I'd been hammering for a second baby when our marriage was in shambles and my mental health was hanging on by a dental-floss-sized string. During our worst fights, Leo had asked me, in French, "to get off his back." In Islamorada, with my anger muddled by the heat and the humidity, I had a revolutionary thought: What if I did?

Just like when an old romantic flame decides to pursue you again once you've finally moved on, my commitment to a cooler, more relaxed vacation attitude resulted in Leo wanting me. When he reached over in our cesspit of a bedroom, the dust-choked air-conditioning blasting to mute the striving of the couple one room over, I sensed that Leo had set his mind to something. "No condom?" I balked. I'd been off birth control for months in an effort to regulate my sleep issues. This was a risk, and it was a big one. But it was also an overture.

Marie-Laure would say that there is no way you can feel fertilization happening during sex, but I am telling you, I felt it. That night, I loamed into a dead sleep of citrus and air freshener, and in the morning, Leo said I'd slept so well, I'd snored. I knew then for sure. The last time I'd gone deep enough into sleep to make that honking sound, I'd been pregnant with our daughter.

Back home on the East Coast, the easy sleep continued and my sadness shifted shape: instead of the blanket of dread that had been weighing down my every thought and action, my unease became unpredictable and exigent. The hunger that turned immediately to revulsion when I tried to quell it, the abdominal bubbling, the thrill of REM sleep: all the signs of pregnancy were back.

Once a plastic stick confirmed that I was, in fact, pregnant, I felt in my gut that we'd taken the wrong path, but because it was something that I'd asked for, it was my mistake to bear. It was a habit of mine: bearing. One time, on a short visit home from France, I was returning from a friend's place in the Adirondacks to attend a goodbye dinner for my brother in Connecticut, who was headed off to an assisted-living college in-state. Though I had the suspicion halfway through my error that I was traveling west instead of east, I drove all the way until I saw a "Welcome to Pennsylvania" sign. When I called home from a gas station to admit that I'd made it to the wrong New Milford, my mother was furious, my brother disappointed, and I burned with shame for weeks. Brendan had been looking forward to saying goodbye to me, and I had let him down—by the time I finally made it home, he was asleep and his bags were packed. But it had been a self-fulfilling prophecy, my failure to reach Brendan—once I suspected I was headed in the wrong direction, I could have turned around, or I could have stopped at a gas station earlier for directions instead of driving on.

A month after our return from Florida, I told Katja that I couldn't continue lessoning with her, that I was pregnant and I needed to think about the baby's health. Unfazed, she told me about a suit that I could wear that would inflate should I be thrown, and it is reflective of how much I wanted to keep going with my lessons that I actually looked this suit up. Privately, I considered how foolish it had been to try and return to riding in the first place. Publicly, I told Katja it wasn't safe, it wasn't reasonable: I wouldn't ride again.

12

WATCH ME

Leo and I stood on the landing of the second floor of our new home in Connecticut, trying to decide where we would put a second child. I had entered my second trimester, so the hypothetical new family member who had been manifesting itself in the form of nausea and debilitating cravings for full-fat cottage cheese was beginning to feel real. The baby would be a baby who would cry out at night and need things, and our house had thin, uninsulated walls. The question of where to put a newborn pressed.

We moved to the doorway of the guest room that I'd slept in (or rather, not slept in) for the months of my insomnia. Thanks to pregnancy, that malady had been quieted. But turning this room into a nursery would mean I wouldn't have a safe place to go when that demon came again, and it meant that we couldn't have sleepover guests of our own. Not that we'd been welcoming a lot of friends out to our house over the past year. Though my depression was untraceable through the lies of social media, in person, I couldn't hide my dull eyes, gaunt face, and weakened, brittle frame.

Though we were nervous and at times overwhelmed with the extra responsibilities headed our way, the pregnancy caused Leo and me to get on the same page. We were like soldiers drafted for a war, resigned to look for opportunities in the new fate that was ours. We drove into the nearest "big town" of Great Barrington to look at a baby bike-seat model that put the child in front of you instead of behind. We looked online at cushy fireside chairs that could seat one adult and two children who wanted to hear a story. When I hit thirteen weeks, we told Nina about the baby.

"I have a sister in there?" she asked, looking at my stomach as if it contained vegetables that she did not want to eat.

"We don't know if it's a sister yet," I said. "A sister or a brother."

"I want it to be a sister."

"You're going to be a great sister," said Leo, and that feeling came, a solid feeling, like the restoration of confidence when a bad storm finally breaks. We could do this. The child might heal us. I looked up at Leo and he smiled at me, and I loved him. We were united. We were back on board.

·

In therapy, Joe was helping me to continue seeing things from a positive point of view. When I worried about the pregnancy, I did so in the language of corporate organizational management: How would our current home structure allow—architecturally—for a new child? How would our roller-coaster finances manage the same?

I was fooling myself, a little, with the HR speak. But I wasn't fooling Joe. He must have realized that I was cloaking real fears under this cold language, because whenever I started to talk about superficial concerns (would our current car suffice, or would we have to get a new one?), he guided me back into the landscape of my childhood, to the way that I had experienced my parents.

Joe wanted to talk about the parts of me that were "in exile" and my "protector parts." I'd never heard this kind of language used in analysis before. It felt as if someone had extended a hand to help me mount a slippery staircase. It was one thing to talk about my feelings, but it was something else entirely to turn around and give those feelings roles.

The part of me that had been gentle was in exile. My playful side was too. The protective sentries I'd built up to guard those exiled parts were perfectionism and self-reliance. Something that really opened me in therapy was when Joe asked if I'd been neglected as a child. I laughed. Neglected? My own pony and a mother who dropped everything for me and a beautiful house with canopy beds for all the sleepovers I wanted, no, I wasn't *neglected.* I remember that Joe's mouth twitched. Okay, so they provided for you materially, he said. What about emotionally?

Tears sprung to my eyes. A memory floated up that I'd thought too long ago and small to break upon the surface. When I was a junior in high school and living with my father, I left a report card on the kitchen counter for him and my stepmother to find. All As (except in math), even some A pluses. Glowing feedback from my teachers, impassioned cries that I had true talent as a writer, that this skill needed to be nurtured.

In the morning, my father already gone for work, I found the report card in the same place with this scrawled on the back: "Courtney this is your's please get Carolyn's skis today + your room Love to see you." I have this report card in a jewelry box, my father's writing clear. It stills me nearly as deeply as it did then, the silence of the empty kitchen, scrubbed clean by a housekeeper, the absence of what I wanted to hear and feel from my father, which was happiness and pride.

Older now than the teenager I was then, I can push aside my hurt to see what my father was trying to say. He wanted me to connect more with my stepmother and show her some respect (a girlfriend of mine had borrowed a pair of her cross-country skis that winter and claimed she couldn't find them at the season's end, an act, yes, of laziness and entitlement on my friend's part but one that was nonetheless raised so many times until my graduation I'm surprised they didn't call the FBI on me); he thought my room was a disaster (it was); he wanted to see me more. At the time, I was more of a tenant than a daughter, living in an actual garret in a castle he'd designed in Conyers Farm. There were so many rooms in that house, my junior year of high school, I spent a long weekend with a boyfriend imported from a Vermont writers' conference that I swear they never met.

And about this "seeing me more" business—this cleaved me apart. The reason my father wanted to "see" me more was that I'd taken to eating "dinner" alone in my bedroom—much earlier than my stepmother and father—and in the eucalyptus-scented office of my therapist, I felt full of rage for the girl who developed anorexia right underneath her parents' eyes. That part of me was in exile. My fun side, my silly side, even my naïveté—I had starved that person out. The bedroom that so bothered my father *was* a mess, a mess of notebooks and diaries in which I was calorie counting and mile tracking and charting everything I ate. I was out the door at 6:00 AM on weekends to go running when most girls my age and in my social class were rolling out of bed at noon to a plate of eggs and bacon. I didn't eat eggs. I didn't eat bacon. I was a vegetarian. And then I was vegan. I was whatever I needed to be to cover up for the fact that I wasn't eating anything at all.

I had never thought about how upset it made me that whether I was at my mother's or my father's, my parents let me hurt myself, how unloved it made me feel, until my therapist asked me if my parents had shown me any neglect. Still to this day, my mother's always on me about how I broke away from her when I was young, and now I want to say, *No: you let me go.* If my own daughter tried to retreat to her bedroom every night at five with a bowl of Grape-Nuts for her dinner (without milk, because milk equals fat, even if it's skim, you never know), I would barricade the dining room until I saw her eat and I would sleep inside her bedroom and I would get a guard dog to bark at her if she tried to empty the wrong parts of herself out into the toilet. I would fight to keep her in front of me. I would ask her why she was trying to injure her one, beautiful body. I would not write a note on her flawless report card indicating that I'd like to see her more.

Yesterday, my daughter—six years old at the time I'm writing this—had a playdate, and her girlfriend came and found me because she said she was feeling sad about something and wanted to talk to an adult. It reminded me of a tendency I had to speak more openly with other people's parents than I did with my own when I was younger. It reminded me of a time when my father asked me if there was any other dad out there as great as him and I answered with the name of a girlfriend's father, and his eyes hardened and he left the room. It reminded me of a time I won a writing contest in ninth grade for a homework assignment that asked us to turn a recurring theme from Greek myths into a story. The themes were up to us to find, and I chose "displacement," the fact that characters—the goddesses, especially—were constantly turning themselves into something other than their human forms to avoid predators. I wrote my homework assignment in the first-person voice of a woman who is raped and turns into a bird so she can get away from her assailant. The story was called "Her," and my English teacher suggested that I enter it in a local contest for student writing, which I ended up winning. At the awards ceremony, I was erroneously given a prize for nonfiction, and after that announcement, I had to read the piece on a stage in front of an audience, and not one member of the jury or my family, not even my beloved grandmother who was present for that reading, asked me why I was writing such a thing at fourteen or if my piece was based on something that I'd actually experienced. It is hard to ask confrontational questions, but it can be harder on the would-be receiver to leave such questions unasked.

Joe's suggestion that I had experienced neglect made me realize that it was valid for me to feel upset, because I had cried out for help when I was younger, and nobody had come.

13

CHROMOSOME 21

A few weeks into my second trimester, I found out my pregnancy wasn't viable, which is a clinical way of saying that our baby died.

The gynecological practice I patronized in Connecticut was a far cry from Marie-Laure's in Paris. And while I knew that in moving back to America, I would lose some of the romance and eclecticism that accompanied many French things, I didn't realize that I would also lose a female doctor who spoke to me as an ally and who knew what it was like to menstruate, to feel soreness in her breasts, to make life and lose life.

On the East Coast, both in Massachusetts and in Connecticut, I had a hard time finding a female gynecologist. I found a compromise in Dr. Habert, who, while male, had a deadpan humor that I thought might replace Marie-Laure's delicious snobbishness.

The practice Dr. Habert worked out of was pretty much the only game in town, and by "in town" I mean the only practice under an hour's drive from our new home in Connecticut. (While our cozy hamlet boasted a general store and a public library, big-league amenities like gynecologists and grocery stores were still a haul away.)

Though the office was a small one with a scenic view, the energy of the place was odd. If I dared ask a direct question ("When should I get a mammogram?"), I was given a blousy answer ("Oh, somewhere after age fourty-five or before fifty, more or less?"), and the only eye contact the medical staff ever made was with my online chart.

So when the results of the genetic screening tests I'd been strongly encouraged to take because of my "geriatric" maternity age were delayed one week, and then yet another week, again, I chalked this up to the fact that this obstetrics practice was always at loose ends. I wasn't worried about what information might have been in those delayed results, because my pregnancy with Nina had been textbook healthy, enjoyable, and fun.

The appointment I'd brought Leo to that day was an ultrasound at which we'd find out the baby's sex. We hadn't told our respective parents about the pregnancy yet, only Nina, and so we'd agreed to announce both the news of our second baby and its purported gender in one go. We'd get out of the appointment around noon, which would be 6:00 PM in France. If we managed to reach them, Leo's mother and father could celebrate with a glass of wine, and my mother, whose greatest joy was grandparenting, would be over the moon regardless of the hour that our phone call reached her.

But the baby wasn't alive. When Dr. Habert came into the radiology room, called there by a screener with a dismal poker face, he told us that it looked like the pregnancy hadn't been vital for at least a week. And I remembered—I remembered how a week earlier I had been biking Nina to her day care and a darkness had come over me, a nausea so compelling it was all I could do not to let all of us—me, the bike, my daughter—crash onto the ground. I fainted on the neighbor's lawn—I wasn't out long, Nina blinking on the grass beside me, still strapped in her bike seat. I walked us home eventually, sat down, and the world spun. But after that, the nausea that had plagued me for months moved on to somewhere else. Mistakenly, I thought that I had entered the healthier, easier part of the second trimester, a period that I'd thrive in, but it was just because the fetus wasn't eating, wasn't growing. The fetus wasn't alive.

Horses are often referred to as "fight-or-flight" animals. That is, they are physiologically wired to react to stressful situations in one of two ways: by staying and fighting, or by fleeing what scares them. When the going gets tough, I have something of the fighter in me, but I think it's an instinct born of cowardice, not courage. A year earlier, after the car accident that, in many ways, had opened the door to my depression, I didn't turn to check on Nina in her car seat beneath the haze of airbag particles; I leapt out of the car and ran to the dazed driver whose faulty turn had caused the accident, screaming about what could have happened to the child I hadn't even checked on. For so long, I had been convinced that terror was everywhere and that my daughter's life was at risk, and this man's miscalculated turn had proved the darkest part of me correct. When I stopped yelling at this poor fellow, I turned back to our demolished car to see Leo cradling Nina—he'd been the one, the father, who had thought of her needs first.

My reaction regarding the news about our baby was also one of rage.

"Is there anything I can do for you?" Dr. Habert asked us, my husband sitting pale-faced on a pullout chair, my ankles clasped in the clutches of the examination stirrups.

"I never got my genetic screening results!" I cried. "They're weeks and weeks late. I need them. I need them, now!"

I was sitting on a bench in our backyard that I'd salvaged from my father's house before he left Connecticut for his mother's native Tennessee in 2007 when I got the doctor's call, only hours later. Although Dr. Habert didn't say that he was calling with good news, his tone of voice was so upbeat that *I'm calling with good news* was what I heard him say.

"The fetus had 99.9 percent Down syndrome," Dr. Habert announced. "Would you like to know the sex?"

Best-case scenario, was what I heard the doctor add. *You really dodged a bullet.* Although he didn't say these things, his relief was so palpable, I hurried the call along because I didn't want his tone to influence the way I absorbed the screening test's results. When we hung up, I stared into the algae of the pond that Leo had been battling with carps and varied chemicals ever since our move, and put my hands over the place where our small, dead son was resting in my stomach.

I thought of my brother, Brendan, in that moment. Though my pregnancy could have miscarried for any number of reasons, the idea that it had happened because of Down syndrome was powerful, as was the fact that my daughter and son would have had the same age gap as my brother and I: five years.

It isn't a good look to fetishize the disposition of a person who has mental and physical handicaps, but everyone who knows Brendan will agree that my brother is a grateful person capable of talking for days about how awesome a lasagna was, or a TV show he likes. He's married now to a woman who bags groceries at the Winn-Dixie near my mother's house in Florida. My brother works as a meet-and-greeter at a nearby golf club, where he welcomes all the regulars with a jubilant "How's it going, champ? You gonna show those holes a thing or two, or what?" My brother wouldn't have gotten himself into a mess like this, because he would have been happy with everything he already had.

The sun rose in the sky and the doctor's phone call sank in, as did the fact that this was it for me—the pregnancy wasn't viable. I did not feel relief and I didn't feel anger; in fact, the anger that had coursed up in me at the doctor's office had completely disappeared. It is hard to talk about this, because I don't consider myself a religious person, but the moment felt religious. Sitting in the sunlight on an inherited bench while the fat frogs leapt and croaked, I vowed not to let this little spirit's life go unrecognized. I could not go on withholding joy from my own life, when there was so much joy right there—there!—to reach out and make mine. He wanted me to be happy. I felt it. I needed to learn to love better. I had to love myself. His death gave me that time.

14

THE FIRST HARLEY

After my parents' divorce and my mother's relocation to a tidy colonial in Old Greenwich, a host of suitors crunched up the gravel driveway to court my mother, one of which was a Harley-Davidson Sportster motorcycle.

Though we'd practically lived on bicycles when we used to vacation as a family in South Carolina, I'd neither seen nor heard anything about my mother lusting after the motorized kind before. But there he was, the Sportster: black leather plush seating, silver chrome and swagger, idling with patient little grumbles to take my mother away. There wasn't any man on that bike waiting for her: she got her motorcycle license and bought the bike herself, joining a mysterious group on Sundays for backcountry rides to a dairy farm upstate. That motorcycle was a ticket, post-divorce, to reinvention, and it was a way for her to get away from my teenage nastiness and my brother's fragile health. For so long, I thought I knew everything there was to know about my mother: she was available, she was generous, she never forgot anything at the grocery store. She was a harbor and a ferry, a self without the self. But this motorcycle went off-script. My mother was a woman, first and second, a grown-ass woman with disappointments and guilty pleasures and needs that I had no idea about, things I'd never thought to ponder. She was a woman out there buying tasseled saddlebags and black leather biking chaps. She was someone whose mind was elsewhere when she returned with her hair in a tangled bird's nest and her wide cheeks pinkened on Sunday afternoons, and because she had access to a dreamland that I was not a part of, on those days I loved her best.

Where did that bike go? It was replaced by a man, eventually, and those Sunday rides stopped. Sometime after the arrival of a blue Volvo belonging to the contractor who would become my stepfather, the Sportster was sold. We would move again, to a lake community this time, where the neighbors sped around in golf carts with coolers full of cocktails, and my mother would purchase his-and-hers scooters that she and her new husband would zip around in until the golf cart proved more practical and those scooters, too, were sold. That house, in New Milford, Connecticut, was mere miles from the dairy barn that my mother used to Sunday out to, which is to say that, in my mind, the independence and fearlessness my mother showed during her Harley days was right there in her grasp. But with a wedding ring back on her finger, my mother started to wife again, this time for a man who worked from home and didn't like her to do anything social without him. If she had to be gone, she would leave him meals labeled "lunch" and "dinner." And then there were her children: I was closing in on myself and declared I wanted nothing from my mother, while my brother was all open arms and IV drip bags that hung above his hospital bed like bloated jellyfish.

My mother sent me a letter this fall, in the midst of the pandemic. A few months earlier, in her Florida enclave, she had contracted the virus that was killing people and closing businesses around the world. She wrote that we could never be sure how much time we both had left, so we needed to get down to it: Why was I so upset with her? Why did I act as if I just didn't like her, all of these long years?

Perhaps this story is my attempt to work out my response. If there is one thing that I am growing sure of in the body that I'm writing from, it is that women deserve to have both a secret inner life and a way to activate and celebrate that life outside the home. Whether it is on a horse or on a motorcycle, in the arms of a stranger at a dance class, equipped with knitting needles or a novel dog-eared to within an inch of its life, we need passions that are ours and ours alone, so that we can be ourselves, instead of somebody else's something: mother, ex-wife, wife.

For me, the realization that I must return to horses—regardless of the time commitment, impracticality, or cost—came under the hands of the doctors, all men, who removed the lifeless fetus from my body with little respect for the person still residing in it.

It was 5:00 AM when Leo and I arrived at the hospital, where we were shown to a private room with the view of the roof running across the hospital's cafeteria and, beyond that, the horizon where the sun would show up soon. The doctor, a man I'd never met before, came in with a coffee stinking of artificial hazelnut and asked if we had questions, nudging my husband before I could answer. "I bet *you* have a lot of questions," he said, to Leo. "Like when you can get back to hanky-panky!"

Later, as I lay on the gurney, a brutish anesthesiologist leaned over to inquire why my eyes were teary, did I have a cold? Angrily, I replied that no, I was sad, and he punched me on the shoulder and said, "Hey! Just make another one!"

I remember yearning for a horse with all the might I had within me when the anesthesiologist said this. Yearning for that power and that synchronicity with an animal who had also been misjudged and mistreated and handled like an ornament. I remember thinking, I am going to gallop over your fucking face, you moron. And then he knocked me out with something that he shot inside my arm, and I was wheeled into a cold room, and then I wasn't pregnant anymore.

15

HIPS LIKE A WHORE

After the miscarriage, I went on a mental health improvement spree. In addition to continuing talk therapy with Joe, I visited an energy therapist in the healing arts capital of Great Barrington to help regulate my cycle: after the pregnancy loss, I was either bleeding all the time or not bleeding at all. I started seeing an acupuncturist, who stuck needles in my anxiety. I bought a ficus plant for my bedroom that I could nourish and watch grow. But the most important decision—and investment—that I made was going back to ride.

The stable where I'd been lessoning before the miscarriage wasn't available to me any longer: Katja's lesson horse had died from Lyme disease complications during my time away, and all the other horses at the barn were leased. After online research and phone calls, I found a new place about twenty minutes from my house called Burr Mountain Farm. What Burr Mountain lacked in amenities, it made up for in heart. Gone were White Bridge's Range Rovers and Escalades parked in front of stalls filled with six-figure dressage mounts: Burr Mountain was a one-ring establishment with clients of the used Subaru persuasion parked alongside mixed-breed rescue horses and a retired draft horse who was quite long in the tooth.

The owner was a single mother named Lainey, a no-nonsense truth teller who let me work against the cost of lessons with barn chores. From the moment I opened the pasture gate to halter a paint horse who was two parts suspicious and one part convinced I had access to his food, I knew I was back in the right place. I could feel the tension in me losing some electricity. My shoulders—raised up to my ears, normally—relaxed, my jaw wasn't as tight. Chickens pecked the packed-dirt parking lot and tore squawking through the outdoor ring at the mere rumor of a bear. There were about eight horses, three full-time boarders, the chickens, outdoor trails. All had health in them.

One thing I loved about Lainey, and would continue to seek out in all the horse people I met, was that she put safety first and airs dead last. She didn't give a rat's ass what brand my helmet was or what clothing I rode in: she wanted me to learn quickly, pay attention, and display common sense. There weren't any ready-to-go lesson horses at Burr Mountain either. Rain, sun, or off-season snow, I had to bring my mount in from its paddock, work the mud out of its coat, pick the manure and earth from hooves without getting my hand stomped, remember where to put the noseband, browband, cheek strap, learn how to get a bit into the mouth of a horse who kept his horse teeth clamped.

Though Lainey could be distant and a little abrasive in the barn aisle, once you were in the riding ring, her teaching talents shone. You would have thought we were training for the World

Equestrian Games from the urgency she showed me. While a stupid mistake might earn me a hollered, "Are you hearing me?!" the
smallest of improvements would get a "YES!" so earth-shatteringly
loud, it was only because of his familiarity with her yelling that
the paint horse didn't spook.

Once I was comfortable with Lainey and Lainey with me, I
asked her if I could bring my daughter along from time to time
to help. With my yearnings for a second child upended, I felt
confident and happy about my three-person family. Knowing it
would be Leo, Nina, and me for the long run reinvigorated my
commitment to my little girl. I wanted to find a way to mother
her that had nothing to do with nagging her to get dressed, to
eat, to bathe, but instead celebrated the fact that as a mother to
a daughter, I might have things to teach her; life experience that
she could either take or not take, but at least learn from.

For so long, I had been thinking of my child as a worthy time
commitment that nevertheless ate into my time. How and when I
wrote, socialized, traveled; it all depended on what was happening
with my daughter. But I was slowly realizing that I could incorpo-
rate my child inside my joys, that if I showed her how to participate
in the things I cared about, she might care about them too. That is
to say, instead of just reading *Harold and the Purple Crayon* for the
thirteenth time that week, I could ask Nina how the story would
be different if the crayon were not purple, if the main character
had been an old woman instead of a little boy. In this way, I could
insinuate how exciting it was to write the stories we read together,
night after night. Show her how the sauce was made.

And I could show her horses, especially at Burr Mountain,
where, as a single mother, Lainey was all about letting caretakers

do whatever they needed to parent and ride, as long as everyone stayed safe. This seemed the way forward for me: not to leave Nina at home because Mama wanted to ride, but to take her with me so she could see why Mama loved to ride so much.

And so I started bringing Nina along to help with my barn chores. Whether Nina was watching hose water spit into a bucket or pushing a pitchfork into a pile of fresh poop, Lainey spoke to her like a small adult who was perfectly capable of understanding why it was dangerous to sneak behind a horse, why you couldn't wave a hoof pick at a horse's face, why you had to yell "Door!" when you came in and out of the barn. She spoke to Nina sternly when she merited it, and kindly when she needed encouragement. It was from watching Lainey with my daughter that I realized that children yearn for discipline and boundaries, and that when "no" is said the right way, it can actually mean it, whereas the "no" that I'd been using was as expansive and porous and flexible as cork.

Saturday after Saturday, I drove out to Burr Mountain with a bag of snacks, extra clothing, and Nina in her car seat, singing in the car. At four years old, she already had the same taste in sugary pop music as I did: catchy refrains, major-to-minor shifts, love songs through and through. Just like me, she loved Taylor Swift and Selena Gomez and Katy Perry and Alicia Keys, and because my French husband, born and bred on electronic music, winced when we played such music at home, it became a ritual of ours to blast this candy in the car.

Once we arrived at the stable, I'd bundle Nina up in whatever the unpredictable weather merited that day, and we'd pull the horses out of their stalls together, me holding the haltered horse with Nina to my left, trudging in our rain boots through the muck to their pastures. After the horses were outside, we'd wheel-barrow out hay flakes that I'd let Nina throw, a task she delighted in as each toss won her a warm eye and a nicker. Then came the dirty work: the shoveling out of nighttime poop and the turning over of horse bedding. Sometimes, I had to climb up a ladder to throw extra bales of hay down, which resulted in protests of hives and scratches on my newly sensitive-to-everything middle-aged skin. When these chores were taken care of, I'd take a break, and Lainey would give me the lesson that I'd earned.

In our lessons, we were focusing on one thing in particular: a dressage concept called "positive tension." Positive tension is about being relaxed but strong, rigid but balanced, supple but determined. In short, it is an enigma that made absolutely no sense to my type A brain. How do you keep your elbows bent when the horse's head is pulling you downward and snapping your arms stick-straight? How do you keep your legs closed on the horse, but your hips open? Your fingers firm on the reins, but your hands soft? Lainey even wanted me to have soft *eyeballs*, but I was supposed to use those same eyes to drive the horse toward whatever point she chose. How do you hold on to that kind of equilibrium? How do you reconcile control and free-spiritedness? Seriousness and joy? This balance seemed impossible, a challenge alpine in scale. It was extra frustrating because I knew that I rode freely as a child. When I was little, it came naturally: the confidence and the easy pleasure to unify with a horse. But it was anything but easy in my adult body. For a few seconds, I'd find that balanced sweet spot, but then it would be gone: the horse would stumble and I'd fall forward—or rather I'd lean too far forward and cause the horse to stumble—or I'd allow something from my outer life to creep into my mind, and my seat, the balanced position that gives riders a fair shot at security, would fall apart. These minute defeats felt impermissible given the little I was doing in the ring. Lainey's outdoor ring was narrower than a tennis court, so it was hard to sustain anything over a brisk trot. It wasn't like I was in danger of being run away with, and yet even at slow gaits I couldn't find the positivity in the tension that I needed. It was just tension.

My frustration mounted. Regardless of the fact that I was freshly back to riding, and that I'd just made and lost a human and had another child playing with Lego BrickHeadz on a bench outside the ring, I felt like maybe I would never master this one essential thing: the marriage between flexibility and conviction that is the essence of a solid seat. My throat was closing, my face burning. Was I going to cry?

"COURTNEY!" Lainey shouted. "You are going to get it! You are going to listen! SHOULDERS LIKE A QUEEN, HIPS LIKE A WHORE!"

This comparison unlocked something for me. It wasn't that Lainey's comment magically corrected my position, but it made me laugh, and in laughing, I unwound. I could see the big picture again—no small feat in a discipline that is about micro-adjustments, micro-twitches, micro-everything. I was there to get better, yes, but it had to be fun first. If I couldn't laugh at myself, I wasn't going to be able to access the relaxation that is such an important part of riding. And there was a lot to laugh about! I was making mistakes, but they were honest mistakes, because I was learning this all over again. I wasn't perfect yet, because maybe I had never been perfect at all.

On my way back into the barn, Nina greeted me in the aisle with one curry comb on her foot, her socks pulled to her knees like shin guards.

"Mama!" she said. "I have a new shoe!"

Her boisterous curls—so blond and wild then—were coiled irrepressibly, and she was pink in the face with pleasure from finally getting to show me the goofy thing she had done.

I know where to go now, I thought on the drive home, Nina's happiness nearly barometric in the air between us. I can be more open. I can enjoy instead of chide, take delight in the small things. I can have the shoulders of a queen and the hips of a person who is in touch with her sensuality, I can. As we wound our way through the backcountry roads singing along to Taylor Swift—my daughter's favorite—we belted out that we would make the moves up as we went.

16

CHRONICLE OF HORSES

As the fallen leaves gathered in hoof tracks crusted with freezing ice, it became clear that I was going to have to find a new barn if I wanted to keep riding through the winter. As wonderful as Lainey was, Burr Mountain's outdoor ring would soon be under snow.

I embarked on a Goldilocks search for a new facility with an indoor ring that would fit my modest budget. It took more than three tries. This one was too precious, this one was too far, this one wanted me to pay a $1,000 entry fee before I even got to ride. Though I bounced around from place to place, there were commonalities: at every barn, the parked cars boasted bumper stickers of the "Not all chicks ride like girls" and "Silly cowboy, trucks are for girls" variety. Riding was an activity that was dominated— with few exceptions—by women young and old.

Many books have tried to unlock the unique bond between horses and women—*Horse Girls,* edited by Halimah Marcus, and *Why We Ride*, edited by Verna Dreisbach, are two favorites (I contributed to Halimah's book, so I'm biased on that one)—but fewer texts explore why a certain kind of woman rides. From barn to barn, I kept meeting women who moved like me: high-strung, hurried, comforted by routine. And though horses need routine too—indeed, they thrive inside it—everyone who knows horses knows that you can't predict a damn thing with an equine. The trail you take every day suddenly has a fallen branch across it that looks like the bogeyman; a plastic bag ghosts through the air from somebody's deli lunch and your horse dumps you at a cross-rail; a rote riding lesson turns into a visit to the emergency room because of the lethal combination of hailstorm and metal roof.

Nervous Women, Nervous Horses: The World's Healthiest Pairing could have been the name of the book I was creating in my head that fall. Why did someone like me, who was generally fearful and pessimistic, feel pulled toward an animal that demanded confidence and optimism? I can't speak for the other women I met at the barns, women who kept on coming back to riding even after their worst-case scenarios had come to pass: broken wrists and shattered clavicles and broken backs and comas. But for me, it was addictive to be participating in something fully physical. For decades, my life—and the way that I supported myself—had been grounded in the cerebral. Reading other people's writing so that my own writing could be better, editing other people's writing once I became skilled at publishing, myself. Writing ad campaigns and marketing copy and website copy and artist statements and whatever paid the bills. I read somewhere that writing burns an excessive number of calories, and it was beginning to feel that way in my late thirties. I was so tired of *thinking* all the time. While I was definitely seeing benefits from talk therapy

(I was feeling less anxious, and was slowly learning that not every challenge in my life necessitated a five-alarm reaction), I was growing weary of thinking and *talking* all the time there, too.

"How many people have been just transformed . . . or come out of the pain because they have something that loves them back and doesn't ask them questions, doesn't ask them to work through it, they're just there?" asks air force veteran Jeannine McDonald in a filmed interview for *Military Times*. "If you've been hurt, sometimes it's harder to be around other human beings—but there's no judgment with a horse," another female rider, Sarah Smith, tells the *Guardian* about her experience with equine therapy, in a 2015 video. "Words are so limiting sometimes."

That fall, I started watching a lot of videos of women talking about their experiences with horses. Oftentimes—most times, actually—they couldn't find the words. There was one video in particular that resonated with me, a reel put together by the alumni of Facilitated Equine Experiential Learning (FEEL), a nonprofit organization that promotes growth and transformation through equine interactions. We meet a few middle-aged women in the video, but it was the forty-four-year-old Carla who stood out to me because her struggles—or at least the struggles she professed to on camera—seemed akin to my own. Spry, polite, and attentive, with an allure of competence, Carla says she considers herself "joyful at heart," but has been knocked off her fulcrum recently. "Right now, I don't know when I'm being authentic and when I'm not being authentic to myself," she admits, staring at the camera as her eyes tear up. "I just lost my internal center. . . . I want to feel connected again to what's right for me."

In the video, the late instructor Wendy Golding—cofounder of the nonprofit Horse Spirit Connections—accompanies Carla into the barn, where she meets six horses of varying sizes, which she must refrain from touching or talking to so that Carla can observe how her energy affects the horses'. Although the animals are calm and inquisitive at first, a large bay horse starts to "weave" when Carla nears his stall. Weaving—the repetitive swinging of the horse's head from side to side—is a stable vice that can be caused by any number of things, but is most commonly prompted by stress. The horse's frantic bobbing is a stark contrast to Carla's humble immobility. Whether the animal has picked up on Carla's disquiet or is feeling this way himself, it's uncomfortable to watch.

"Learning about yourself in the presence of a horse can move you along in your own self-discovery about what makes you tick, and we as humans seek that naturally," comments Alison Sittek, a FEEL Alumni member, about the connection that Carla would later form with another horse, a big stallion named Thor. Placed with him in a spacious indoor ring, Carla is asked to approach the horse up until the point where she feels his need for space. Off a lead line, without assistance from the trainer, Thor does the same for Carla, approaching her and then rethinking things when he is about ten feet away. The two eventually end up in close proximity to each other with Thor breathing protective halos behind Carla's neck. "I was hoping I could get close to him," Carla admits after the exercise, "but never in my dreams I thought I could lean on him. You know that moment where you can let go because somebody has your weight?"

Night after night I watched videos like this, researched "positive tension" and spinal "powerlines," scanned horse sale sites the country over looking for a soul mate. Without a stable that I felt comfortable at—a homey place like Lainey's where I could bring my daughter—my horse obsession was turning into an addiction that was pulling me away from my family instead of bringing me closer to them. There was a Bonnie "Prince" Billy song called "Horses" I turned to that autumn whose lyrics argued that the singer wouldn't worry about "disappearing into the night" if he could spend all his time with horses. Which made me wonder: Was the singer no longer worried about disappearing because horses quelled that specific fear of his? Or was he saying that the disappearance itself was aspirational, the act of vanishing, the dream?

I wanted to be around horses all the time, learn more about them, learn how to be a better rider, but these wants were so far-ranging, they shot out across the hemisphere, leaving me listless and depleted. I fervently researched horse breeds I was only vaguely acquainted with—Gypsy Vanners, Icelandic horses— convinced that if I identified what my perfect horse was, I would also identify what I was meant to do when I was on it.

I wanted, wanted, wanted with no specific goal in sight. Most active riders are working to perfect a specific discipline: this specificity was missing from my life. At Lainey's, she'd only taught dressage. At another barn I'd tried, it was group lessons in the walk, trot, canter. I'd tried some jumping lessons, which I'd loved, but it was hard to find a trainer who would teach an adult to jump without introducing pressure to participate in horse shows. I loved trail riding and imagined I might excel at eventing, which involves racing around an outdoor jumping course, but none of the facilities let riders take out a horse they didn't own: the risk of injury to the horse and rider was too high.

Each night as I disappeared into a world of online articles and forums, I would tell myself that I didn't have to choose a specific discipline to identify as a rider. After all, people who like to cook prepare all sorts of meals. Passionate readers devour memoir, fiction, poetry. Visual artists work in so many different mediums that "mixed media" is a genre.

But then the morning would come, and my benevolence would be curbed. I needed a focus for this energy, something to work toward. I sat down and assessed what I loved most about being on horseback. I liked riding one-handed, I liked changing gaits, I liked to turn quickly, and I loved being around other riders and their horses in the ring. On the ground, I adored horse contact, and I loved to groom. With these preferences on paper, I saw an answer in their sum, an answer that made no sense whatsoever for my thirty-eight-year-old self. I had never been a natural athlete, I wasn't in great shape, I was a mother to a young child, and I was supposed to be writing books, so why in the hell was I considering looking into one of the most dangerous sports there was? But the idea had been planted. And so I asked the most knowledgeable and connected of my teachers a question that would change the course of my entire year. Did she know anybody who might teach a beginner polo?

17

POLO–THE COLOGNE

Although nobody in my family played polo growing up or knew anyone that did, the trappings and insignia of the sport were all over my house. In the 1980s Greenwich of my childhood, my father's aesthetic ruled, a randy mix of Adirondack camp style and the smooth operating of Sade, all done in Ralph Lauren.

Because most of the pillows, throws, and blankets in our house actually did come from the Ralph Lauren brand, I grew up seeing that polo player logo on everything we owned. Additionally, my father never left the house without his Ralph Lauren Polo cologne on, so the look and smell of that illustrated polo player permeated my childhood.

What's more, an actual polo field demarcated the difference between "Mom's house" and "Dad's house" when I was growing up. The Conyers Farm development my father moved into sits on the border between New York and Connecticut, and is known for quite a few things: the fact that it was founded by the publishing magnate Peter Brant, that Brant is married to the supermodel

Stephanie Seymour, of whom Brant commissioned the life-sized nude bust called *Trophy Wife* that I'd told my husband about—and also for the fact that it boasts a polo club.

Although the Greenwich Polo Club is a hot spot for the shift dress set today, the club was basically defunct when I lived at my father's, the field more of a depot for Peter Brant's outdoor sculptures than an active playing field. On weekends, I would take my spray-painted bicycle to that verdant swath, scrambling up into the empty bandstand to scour the property's tree line for errant polo balls. The clubhouse itself was so underused that I had my thirteenth birthday party inside it—a herd of nervy just-teens standing around listening to the Sinéad O'Connor and Tiffany cassette mix I had mastered for the occasion; pretzel rods in plastic bowls; the heartthrob of the moment, Brian Shepard, causing a scandal by smoking a cigarette out back.

On the rare occasions when there were people actually practicing polo on the field, I never imagined myself being one of the players. If anything, I spent those lonely explorations pretending to be the horse. At ten years old, I was about three years out from learning that I could control what my body looked like by what I put (or didn't put) inside it, and I was developing fast. I was taller, curvier, bustier than other girls, and PE class was a nightmare. On more than a few occasions, I had to face off against a battalion of fifth graders who had decided I was ready for a bra; a humiliation that still burns when I revisit it. I was uncomfortable in a body that felt both cumbersome and unruly. At that time, the only "sport" I excelled at was piano: my tiny wrists and long fingers made more sense curled over ivory keys than they did around the field hockey sticks that my friends wielded with élan.

When I graduated from high school and accordingly left home, the polo club and Ralph Lauren polo player logo became insignia of my past, semiotics devoid of meaning and value at my liberal arts college, where my classmates would rather be smeared in the massive bowl of jelly by the cafeteria bagel bar than be seen in a polo shirt. After college, I moved to France: the horses, the smell of my father's cologne, all of this, long gone. It wasn't until I confronted the list of things I liked to do on horseback decades later that I thought of polo again.

Whether polo originated in Persia or in China is a point of contention among historians and archaeologists alike, but barring any further evidence unearthed to the contrary, both parties agree that polo is the oldest equestrian discipline and competitive team sport. It is also one of the hardest to break into. One can't learn polo just anywhere: a certain kind of facility is needed, and a certain kind of horse. I had never seen a polo club or heard about one anywhere in my new town, and though I'd met all different kinds of competitors in my born-again-rider adventure, I hadn't heard a word uttered about the sport. And yet, the teacher of a womens-only riding group I'd recently joined had a name for me: Mark Gomez. She wrote down his landline on a scrap of paper with a Sharpie pen. "He's the only one I know from that world," she said, shrugging with a definitive energy that made it clear that it was Mark, or nothing else.

18

MI PEQUEÑO PONY

Violent, excessive, expensive, elitist, notoriously hostile to "the second sex"—none of the negative characteristics of polo were on my mind when I drove out for my first lesson with Mark Gomez on a chilly afternoon. The trees were orange and yellow in the sun, the sky was blue as a gift box. Something had called me to this sport, and my car pulled me like a magnet to the person who said that he could help.

"I can't offer you much," Mark had said on the telephone. "I just have a round pen. And a decent pony. And I won't charge you for the first lesson. We need more women in this sport."

In one of my favorite novels, *Madame Bovary*, the main character, Emma (who becomes a serial cheater during a time period when adultery was punishable by death for women), is driven to her first dalliance after the excitement and freedom she experiences from her inaugural horseback ride. Everything is romantic and bucolic and appealing: the fragrant pastures, the innocent grass, the pretty tufts of cloud.

I felt similarly wide-eyed that day at Mark's farm. A lot of horse farms in Connecticut are manicured to a fault: the grass mowed, the shutters freshly painted, the mounts gleaming and protected under the latest in horse blankets and bell boots, their ears pricked with a high and nervous look. Mark's farm, to the contrary, was tousled and enchanting. A simple four-stall barn sat next to his back patio, where the arms of an electric grill flapped in the light breeze. Wildflowers yellowed in the back pastures where quarter horses roamed, and the pony he had promised me was done up in western tack. I felt all-American. Patriotic. I'd unleashed my inner cowgirl.

That polo pony was the first quarter horse I'd come into contact with since I'd returned to riding. If ever there was a creature staunchly resigned to its fate, it is the quarter horse. The little bay in the round pen had all the enthusiasm of a public school bus driver on a November dawn: she was going to take me where I needed to go, and she would do it safely, but she wasn't going to like it.

It didn't matter. From the minute Mark handed a fifty-one-inch mallet to me in that suede saddle, I was downright hooked. It's counterintuitive to people used to riding with two hands, but I felt so much safer with the reins gripped in my left hand and something heavy in my right. At that time, I had a tendency to "death grip"—squeeze the reins too hard, effectively trying to balance myself off the horse's mouth—a bad habit that horses usually react to with increased speed, head tossing, or an earnest attempt to get you off their back. With both reins in my left hand and something anchoring my right, I found that I was able to sit back more easily in my natural seat, and I couldn't balance off the horse's mouth, because static balance wasn't the point. In polo, you are up out of your seat almost all the time. Being out of your seat is aspirational, and you can forget about sitting pretty with your legs at such and such a degree to the girth: in polo, you are pivoting right or pivoting left, you're standing up above the horse and swinging a mallet backward, you're gripping with your knees (a practice that causes blood to freeze in the veins of dressage riders), you are moving all the time. This was dirty, dirty riding at the breakneck speed of a slow trot in a pen. "Eyes on the ball, connect with the ball," Mark said, in a drawl I couldn't place. "You have to get up out of the saddle to swivel and hit, so you don't hit the horse."

The lesson lasted nearly ninety minutes, and looking back now from a place where I'm more informed about the going rate for private polo lessons, I can say that Mark Gomez is a saint. Although each micro-movement felt to me like I was on the cusp of absolute and limitless self-discovery, a stiff lady swatting around at immobile balls on a nearly immobile horse is what it must have looked like to a polo player like Mark. When our lesson was over, my wrist was shaking so violently I couldn't text Leo to tell him that I was coming home. "I'm hooked!" I claimed. "Well, that's kind of a problem," Mark replied. He explained that he had the round pen and a fifty-acre open pasture, an upgrade that I wasn't ready for as the horses could take off. I needed to learn on an enclosed field or in an arena, but with October nearly upon us, we were almost out of polo season, so there wasn't anywhere that I could go to learn. "You'll have to call Victor," Mark said. "But he might not be around."

And so it was that I received another number for another man to see about a horse. Victor, Mark said, was the barn manager at an upstate New York polo club called Paugussett Valley, and he could give me a lesson in the arena they had there. Too scared to ask what such a lesson might cost, I pivoted and asked Mark if it was folly to pursue polo if I didn't have a lot of cash. "Let's just say that nobody quits polo once they start," said Mark, his lips curling in a grin. "You either get sick, go broke, or you die. Nobody just *stops*."

•

As an artist, I am driven by the private: secret worlds and secret thoughts and secret dreams inside my head. When I look back now on the year of my unraveling, I think one of the precipitating factors was how exposed I had become. During my two pregnancies, my body was poked and prodded and looked into all the time. My blood was taken from me, analyzed. My urine, decoded, too. There were so many cooks in the corporal kitchen: even my email inbox was pinging me to let me know how much weight I should have gained by this date and by that one, that my fetus was the size of a lemon, a mango, a papaya now.

And at thirty-seven, I could no longer consider my writing— an emotional safe house for so long—private, either. Although I was fortunate to have a second book deal, writing fiction under contract was something I'd never done before, and I took to it like a horse with an uncomfortable new bit. There were all these check-ins: my agent and my editor wanted to—no, they had a *right* to—see new pages, so all of a sudden, my creative process, which had been so intimate and solitary, was something for the gatekeepers to weigh in on and assess.

In the domestic sphere, I didn't have a lot of secrets either: we were potty-training Nina and getting her to eat more complicated solids. Dinner talk was fecal matter and constipation, not seduction or romance. Where was my inner life, my fantasies? Overtaxed, understimulated, I didn't even have the energy to have erotic dreams. There was no private tent left in my mind, everything was just an open, barren gape.

Many years later, I would watch a French film called *Sink or Swim*, about a depressed, unemployed father named Bertrand who goes out for his provincial town's male synchronized swim team despite the fact that he has never shown an interest in or a talent for the sport before. Bertrand's friends and family members start to make fun of this new pastime to his wife, Claire, saying that the sport is effeminate, that there are rumors about Bertrand's sexuality, that he must be going mad. But Claire says nothing to her husband, suspending judgment until she accompanies him to a performance of the team he wants to join. From a set of nearly empty bleachers, Claire first watches the out-of-shape middle-agers launching themselves around in the water with little skill or grace. Then she shifts her attention to the husband sitting beside her, a man who has not smiled or laughed in over a year. Bertrand's eyes are shining. His face is glowing. He is witnessing something that Claire can't see, but what she can see is that it's helping him. The next time a nosy neighbor criticizes her husband's newfound passion, she gives the woman an epic dressing-down. She is proud of her husband. She is happy for him.

This character, Bertrand, finds his secret place beneath the unemployment offices he is visiting and the disability checks he is collecting, a place out of reach to the people who look down on him and undervalue his potential. For me, pursuing polo also gave me back my secret storage: a place to dream and scheme that belonged to no one else. I didn't know what I was getting myself into with this polo research, but I did know that it was mine. I made phone calls in my office with the door closed, arranged meetings when my daughter was in daycare, looked at quarter horses online. As for Leo: much like Claire, who had a husband who was smiling again, Leo had a wife who was sleeping through the night and had ceased biting people's heads off. Nina had started scribbling horse shapes on our grocery lists, and I had in-jokes with my daughter ("Did you hear about the man who ate six horses? The doctor said he was stable!") for the first time in so long.

When I told Leo that I was going to track down a man named Victor at a polo match because I couldn't get him on the phone, and would Leo like to come on this reconnaissance mission with me, my love for him ignited because he did not ask me why I needed to do this thing that was so out of character. He did not point out that polo was physical and dangerous and that I was mostly sedentary; he did not say it was expensive and that I was a spendthrift; he simply said, okay, that could be fun. Watching a polo game with me and Nina, sure, that could be fun. And so, on a sunny Saturday with the perfect mix of summer haze and autumn coolness, we set out for the rolling hills of upstate New York.

•

Founded in the 1890s as a massive dairy operation, the Paugussett preserve is dotted with hauntingly large red-roofed dairy barns that were renovated in the aughts and saved from disrepair. Today, many of these structures house the polo strings of members and visiting players who populate the area from May to late September. All the barns stand empty for the months outside of polo season; target practice for the winter crows.

Even though I would drive up its rambling entrance many times over the coming year, I never numbed to the beauty of Paugussett. Squat and freshly painted cottages bordered the main entrance, standing watch over the westernmost polo field where the important games were played. Past this were cattle belonging to a separate ranching operation that shared some of Paugussett's land, the gloomy, massive bodies of the Angus bulls and the doom calls of their bellows adding to the otherworldly atmosphere that reigned over the club.

Rumbling into the facility itself on a road of dirt and pebbles, I'd drive through voluminous clouds of dust from the exercise track, where players tired out amped-up ponies pre-match and grooms exercised their bosses' mounts at dawn. Beyond this lay the gated arena where players would scrimmage, stick-and-ball their ponies, or try out new polo prospects in an enclosed space. The four-story ruins of a cement slaughterhouse overlooked this arena, a harrowing sight that recalled the "ruin porn" photography of shuttered amusement parks and roller coasters, stilled.

Past this blight lay the individual barns of the *patrons*, the deep-pocketed, mostly male individuals who pay to sponsor a team and play alongside professionals through a season. These barns housed the two dozen or so horses belonging (or rented) to the patrons, the horses' flanks branded with provenance tattoos. Because a polo pony's mane is shaved to keep it from getting tangled in tack and their tails are braided and tied up for matches, it's hard to tell the armies of finely muscled ponies apart. As we drove in, confusedly searching for the "field 4" I'd noted from the club's calendar, we had to stop to let grooms gallop by on steeds they were rushing out to players; grooms hot-walking huffing ponies with furious nostrils; barn managers whizzing by on four-wheelers with bouquets of extra polo mallets clattering in rear racks.

As I watched the game with my family on the abandoned bleachers because we hadn't known to bring the collapsible chairs and blankets that the people in the know had, I tried not to equate the sport I was spectating with one that I myself felt driven for some reason to try. After all, these men (all men) were galloping up and down a massive field at speeds that made my hands clench—my experience to date with "speed" was the minute of solo canter time allotted during my group lessons with sexagenarian women who drank decaf tea on ice. I was a curious and perseverant born-again rider, but I wasn't any good yet. It appeared to me from watching the men smashing into the horses galloping beside them, reaching across their running horses to hit a ball backward, sitting through a rear, slamming a three-inch ball at thirty-five miles an hour, that "good" didn't suffice. I'd have to be great.

At halftime, a period where, at showier venues, women in ill-chosen heels and men in yawning khakis take to the field to boozily stomp divots, I set out to find Victor. I asked the nearest spectator if he knew anyone by that name, and hit bingo right away. I was pointed to a mounted figure in the middle of the field. "He's the *umpire?*" I balked, registering that the impromptu meeting I was after was going to be even more awkward than I could have imagined.

Instructing my daughter to stay behind with her papa because I had no idea, in truth, how long a polo halftime lasted, I marched out to the middle of field 4. The umpire saw me coming, head cocked, his large horse catching its breath through blood-red nostrils. "Victor?" I confirmed when I got close enough to see that he was smiling. "I'm Courtney? Mark Gomez sent me?"

"*¡Mamacita!*" Victor cried, throwing his arms out. "We have been waiting for you!"

19

THESE VIOLENT EXERCISES

In polo, as in all other aspects of life, women have had to fight like hell to play equal with the boys. Despite the fact that ancient Persian and Chinese works of art and literature refer to women excelling at the sport (a painted pottery figure from the Tang dynasty shows a mounted female polo player reaching across her galloping horse for the infamous "nearside" shot 1,500 years ago), when polo was brought to the West from India in the early 1900s, motivated female players had to make great strides to break into the sport.

Regardless of whether women had the strength and mindset for contact sport, the question floated as to whether women should be seen exercising at all. "The prettiest woman in the world loses her beauty when at these violent exercises," the journalist Eliza Lynn Linton wrote in an article called "The Wild Women as Social Insurgents" in 1891. "Hot and damp, mopping her flushed and streaming face with her handkerchief, she has lost that sense of repose, that delicate self-restraint, which belongs to the ideal woman." It is worth noting here that Linton was the first female paid journalist in all of Britain. A groundbreaking feminist anti-feminist, it would seem.

And if one agreed to let them sweat, it boggled the mind to consider how female polo players should be *clothed.* Women were still riding sidesaddle, and it was out of the question that they appear in pants. Photographs from one of Europe's first women-only polo matches at the London Ranelagh Club in the summer of 1905 show the female players in high-necked, long-sleeved blouses, full skirts, and *boater hats* instead of helmets. It took over ten years until a particularly wild woman known to the press only as "Mrs. Hitchcock" shirked tradition, put pants under a skirted pinafore, donned an actual helmet, and mounted her horse astride for a saucy match in Narragansett, Rhode Island, in 1913.

The suffragette movement allowed women to get the vote and go about in trousers, but for would-be polo players, it was nearly impossible to find a way to play. At the turn of the century, some American colleges had started to adopt polo programs, but these were run by the US Army, and seeing that women were barred entrance to military service academies until 1976, you can imagine how eager the army was to teach ladies polo in the 1920s. The governing male bodies of the United States Polo Association (USPA) weren't keen on mentoring women players, either. When a certain Dorothy Wheeler (who would go on to become the chair of the Pacific coast's Women's Polo Association in 1934) wrote to USPA secretary treasurer F. S. O'Reiley in 1932 for assistance forming a women's league, his response was curt: "Polo is not a women's game."

Although there were a handful of intrepid women playing in the early twentieth century (the brilliant sportswoman and real estate developer Marion Hollins was tearing up polo fields around the country as early as 1920), the USPA doggedly refused to extend membership to female players, responding in 1934 to yet another of Dorothy Wheeler's entreaties that "it was not the policy of this Association to make any attempt to identify itself with women's polo."

It would take the singular talent and sheer tenacity of the California-born Sue Sally Hale—"Sue Sal" to her confidants—to break this gender barrier. From age eleven on, Hale had been binding her breasts, netting her hair, and painting on a mascara mustache to join the polo-playing gentlemen of the Pacific Palisades. For two decades, she braved opposing team members who refused to play against her, relentless hypocrisy from the teammates she scored goals for, and countless injuries from riding whatever was thrown her way until finally, in 1972, she was just too damn good to say no to anymore, and Sue Sally Hale became the first female member of the United States Polo Association.

Sue Sally Hale's trailblazing eased the way for her equally talented daughter, Sunset "Sunny" Hale, who won the first USPA Open Women's Polo Championship in 1990 with her mother, her sister Stormie, and her French teammate Caroline Anier. In 2000, Sunny made history again when she was paid to join the US Open team sponsored by Tim Gannon of Outback Steakhouse. The first woman ever to take the field as a paid polo professional at that level of competition, Sunny was on the team that won.

Today, women represent the fastest-growing polo sector in the world, and female players make up 40 percent of the USPA's membership. The story of women breaking into polo is one that heartens me, because men and women had to come together to fight prejudice: women couldn't have broken the gender barrier without the help of a few good men, and the dawdling, old-school USPA would have caved in on itself by now if it weren't for the renewed energy and resources that women are pouring into the sport. I know I'm not the only woman who got a leg up on a polo pony because of a man who put sportsmanship before gender.

I had one lesson with Victor before Paugussett shut down for the season. He put me on a pregnant chestnut mare named Thunderosa who had more patience and languor than her name suggests. We were in the arena with the crumbling concrete slaughterhouse as a backdrop; it was early morning, the grass fields still drenched with dew, the fog so thick over the mountains that you had to know they were there to believe they were.

At the club I play at now, sometimes while I'm going to fetch the wraps and boots and battery of other things you need to prep a polo pony, I'll hear my coach shout out, "Yes! YES! GOOD!" from the arena, a sure sign that she's giving a polo lesson to a newbie. I'll take a few minutes to linger in the viewing room to watch, smiling at the mother or aunt or grandparent who is inevitably also there. It never looks like much, someone's first polo lesson, but I know how it feels, and I love to watch the children leaning halfway over a moving pony to connect with a small ball on the ground, then sitting back and doing it again, flabbergasted with delight that they haven't fallen off.

If you consider trotting in a circle on a pregnant mare after a neon-orange ball under the supervision of a jocular Dominican with a bum right leg "polo," then I fell in love with polo at

Paugussett shortly after dawn. Five months earlier, five years earlier, I never would have guessed that I, a lifetime avoider of contact sports and spontaneity, would be at a polo lesson with an actual polo player at my side.

But what pulls us out of darkness can be surprising. I know a woman my age who fought her way out of depression by studying tango. She's made a life out of the dance form now, organizing trips to Buenos Aires for single women every year—not, as you might be thinking, to help them partner with a handsome Argentinean, but rather to teach them how to harness the power and potential that are already inside them, a practice she has trademarked as Pussywalking. Another female friend discovered after her husband finally succumbed to the cancer she'd dropped everything to help him beat—that he'd been cheating on her for the last decade of their marriage. She tackled her rage by throwing herself into the raising of chickens and an adopted Weimaraner puppy named Moon, who wanted to eat her chickens, complicating things. But love is complicated.

Sitting on a battered green director's chair after my lesson while Victor put polo wraps around my trembling wrists, I felt positively giddy, even though my hands were shaking from having gripped the heavy mallet too hard.

"I love it, I really love it!" I said. "When can I come again?"

"Oh, you come in spring!" said Victor, cheerfully. "We all fly tomorrow!"

I knew this, of course I knew that polo on the East Coast did not take place on snow. Wellington, Florida, was where most of the American polo world would decamp to until the ground thawed, but Victor would be heading home to the Dominican Republic, where he had cattle, children, and nephews waiting on him. He hugged me, told me he'd be back soon, and promised that he'd call me when he was.

20

NEW BEGINNINGS

The Hadley Velvet Camisole was updated with a chunky pendant, a roomy Nepalese wool cardigan, perfect-fitting blue jeans, and frisky ankle fringe boots. The model wearing these clothes was ethnically ambiguous, lanky in an exciting way, a forty-year-old who looked twenty in her makeup-free makeup. She was leaning against an artfully distressed midcentury table where a bowl of pastel-colored chicken eggs sat next to linen napkins. Behind her, the open prairie swayed in never-ending waves of grain, and the purple mountains' majesty rose up close behind.

Robert Redford's Sundance catalog had been a part of my life since my father and stepmother got married: they were fervent devotees of the western chic the brand expounds. But because I'd recently bought something from the Sundance website for my stepmother's birthday, the catalog was now showing up at my house too. Growing up, I'd found the lace and frill ridiculous and posturing, but ever since I'd been exposed to the polo way of riding, the catalog's New Beginnings Mandala Necklace and River

Secrets Belt called out to me with a siren song of reinvention. If I dressed western, and accessorized western, surely I could manifest my way into meeting a western horse.

The language of polo is Spanish, and the Western world has held on hard and fast to the narrative that it was the Spanish who brought horses to mainland America. Ironically enough, Western technology is proving this to be a fallacy. In 2019, the Lakota/Nakota/Cheyenne scholar Yvette Running Horse Collin worked with the University of Alaska Fairbanks' Indigenous Studies program to finish a groundbreaking dissertation that uses DNA evidence, historical documents, and oral history to suggest that horses were not "introduced" by the Spanish to Native people in the fifthteen century—but were already a deeply important and embedded part of Native culture. "Europeans are still credited for bringing the horses and introducing them to Native people. What does that mean?" Collin asked in an interview with *Indian Country Today* that same year. "They are telling us over and over again that anything that they consider to be of value in our cultures is still 'derivative' of theirs." A Blackfoot (Niitsitapi) tribal member interviewed for Collin's dissertation added, "We have calmly known we've always had the horse, way before the settlers came."

While I don't know where Robert Redford comes down on the horse-in-Native-culture debate, his catalog's overtures to the American horse's origin story can be appropriative and hammer-headed. And yet. As someone who always felt terribly basic in my Caucasian skin, overeager to align myself with the foreign students in my high school and quick to major in a language that wasn't mine in college, Sundance's hodgepodge of multicultural, pseudo-spiritual products was alluring and persuasive. If I owned the Jackie Earth and Sky Jeans with their cascading brocade, surely someone would appear out of nowhere with a quarter horse in hand that would elevate all the equestrian potential that I had inside. And while the La Vida Ruana Poncho would earn me a lot of laughs, the last laugh would be mine, because warmly cloaked inside its cotton heft and tassels, I would be recharged.

I did not succumb, though, to the catalog's entreaty that I buy these things online. Though I did not know what "real" polo would cost me, should the invitation to play again ever come my way, I was savvy enough to know that it didn't make a lick of sense to be spending money on three-figure belts and shawls. But that didn't mean I could resist the pumpkin spice insistence to change my style up for fall. Taking a cue from the Sundance ladies, I sped to the Goodwill two towns over to hunt down embroidered blouses and fitted bolero jackets, a belt that I could get excited about winding through a pair of weathered pants. Though I'd never been a blue jeans person, I could become a jeans person for polo. After all, jeans were the only garment that would allow me to get off my rescued mustang in order to serve mezcal margaritas and homemade jalapeño cornbread to my ranching friends.

The fall of 2016 was also the time that I developed an obsession with Delfina Blaquier, the Argentinean socialite and former high jumper married to the polo player and Ralph Lauren spokesman Nacho Figueras. With the advent of social media, Delfina (mother of four, businesswoman, horse breeder, workout fanatic, and gorgeous fashion darling) had all the credentials to be an Instagram influencer, and influence me she did. I watched videos of her riding bareback with her four adorable children through the Argentinean Pampas, exercising polo ponies (bareback, *claro*) on the Figuerases' private racetrack, tying a tasseled belt around roomy white gaucho pants to go out to a party. I watched her drink and swallow the glass of room-temperature limeade that she drank every morning before *doing any other thing* because, I don't know, it kept her face unlined. Delfina and Nacho's horses didn't live in stables, they lived in concrete outdoor cubes inspired by the groundbreaking Mexican architect Luis Barragán. The older children played polo with their father—the littlest daughter, five years old at the time, raced around the property on a pony using only a sheepskin bareback pad, her blond hair trailing behind her in the breeze.

Other than my beloved blue eyeliner, I have never been a big makeup wearer, and I'm not fussy about skin care. I remember horrifying a French friend's mother in my twenties when she asked me what I washed my face with, and I answered, "Soap?" In high school, I moisturized exclusively with suntan lotion because I loved the summer smell. A long-term birth control regimen had kept my skin more or less pimple-free through my adulthood, and though there were aspects I didn't love about my face (my nose was as sharp and petulant as something out of a Roald Dahl book, my freckles had congealed into almond-colored splotches), it was the face that I'd been given, and I'd never thought to change it, until I hit middle age.

I was thirty-six when I first noticed the lines around my mouth, crevices I'd won from second-guessing and doubting and worrying the small things. I peered closer into the bathroom mirror at the suspect wrinkles. They were so deep and visibly entrenched that at first I thought the skin there had been stained, or that my epidermis was still carrying the imprint of a pillow. My

French mother-in-law was in the house with us the week I found these little devils, and I was so confident that the markings must be temporary, I went into the kitchen to reveal them to her, confident that she would cup my chin and say, *Chérie, there's nothing there.* But the next morning I went for a run, and when I came up to my bedroom, there was a chubby pot of wrinkle cream waiting on my mattress. I should have caught this whole thing earlier, I remember thinking. I should not have said anything about the new lines on my face. Now everyone knows that something has changed inside of me. Now the eyeless thing has been spotted edging from its cave.

When I stopped sleeping, I went out of my way to avoid photographs and mirrors, but now that I was sleeping again and had enough energy to pick up my life's pieces, I confronted my reflection. And what I saw was a woman whose face was stamped with nasolabial lines demarcating her youth's end. I could not stop seeing them, massaging them, putting oils into them, trying everything and anything to make them go away.

Inspired by Delfina, I started drinking tepid water in the morning with hardened limes inside. I bought an expensive mix of drinkable collagen powder that tasted like socks that had fermented inside a dog's intestinal tract. I held wet black tea bags against my eyelids. Made puckering fish sounds to stimulate the muscles in my face.

With a belly full of shame, I asked the acupuncturist I'd been seeing to help me with anxiety to start needling my nasolabial folds, and I even made a Botox consultation with a doctor I found online in New Haven. I was given a consultation appointment four months in the future, and I kept the appointment a secret, as I kept it a secret that I'd made the call at all. I ordered a jade roller that was a cheaper knock-off of the roller Gwyneth Paltrow recommended on her lifestyle site, Goop, and when my daughter used it in imitation of me and dropped it on the floor, shattering its smoothness, it was a challenge not to cry. The efforts I had been putting into developing my riding abilities were now being channeled into my appearance, not the best turn of events as riding had me out in the world and physical, while the appearance fixation had me in front of my computer, staring into the void of internet tutorials and Googling "face sag."

But I truly felt that if I could correct my marring wrinkles, I would feel whole and present again, and would be able to *be* present too. Because I was struggling on that front again. With no more men to see about a horse, I was funneling my energy into discovering the root of my physical shortcomings, which was a sorry use of my free time and a terrible example for my daughter. In front of her sweet face, I was constantly on my phone researching "collagen-boosting vegetables" and "natural face massage," spinning out into a galaxy of self-obsession where I floated without purpose. I couldn't concentrate. I couldn't prioritize. I actually fooled myself into thinking that this dermatological research was important. Leo and I started fighting again. My daughter was growing impatient with me, whiny. She wanted my attention— needed it—but instead, I chose my phone.

Thankfully, about two weeks into my new obsession, I got a call that cut this nasolabial gazing short.

21

THE SECOND HARLEY

There had been a man at my arena polo lesson with Victor, an older retiree named Jay, who, while not a polo player, liked to hang around and help out with the horses. He was an amateur photographer, and he had taken pictures of me in the arena on the pregnant mare. At the end of the lesson, I'd given Jay my number so he could text me photos of my first real *moving* polo lesson, outside of a round pen. In late October—after sending on those pictures—he called to tell me that he had a friend near my town, in Goshen, who wanted to start a polo club at a riding facility called Pie Hill. He bet that his friend might have a horse that I could practice on until Paugussett opened again in May.

I had two lessons with this mystery man, Alfonso, the first of which was on a former racehorse named Dark As Day, whom Alfonso called "DD." It didn't matter what the horse was called: he was strong-willed, mouth-sensitive, and too much horse for me. Clearly disappointed by my risk aversion, Alfonso let me switch out for his mount at our second lesson. Smaller, fatter, and not too keen on polo, Harley was a quarter horse that Alfonso's wife, Marcy, had had for many years. But my performance on Harley was equally lamentable—Alfonso must not have believed me when I'd told him on the phone that I was a "total beginner," because he was exasperated by my inability to hit a small ball at a gallop. To save face, a head injury, and this man's time, I asked whether there was a world in which I could pay to ride Harley on my own for a while, and just work on my riding skills before we started lessoning again.

Alfonso and I had just entered an agreement that this would be not only possible but preferable when the polo tack room was robbed. Showing up one afternoon to inaugurate my solo apprenticeship with Harley, I saw that every single item—all of the beautiful white mallets with their heads stamped with black numbers, the glistening saddles and complicated polo bridles—everything was gone. Harley wasn't gone, but everything I needed to ride him was.

"Marcy?" I answered timorously when she returned my call. Although I would later find out that the barn belonged to Marcy, and had before her marriage to Alfonso, I hadn't had much contact with Harley's owner yet. I was nervous. Although I'd been vigilant with the tack room key that Alfonso had given me, mostly because I felt proud to have been given it at all, it was possible—definitely possible—that I'd left the door unlocked.

"I'm so sorry," I said into the phone, "but I think that you've been robbed! There's nothing in the tack room. Everything is gone!"

"Oh," Marcy said, calmly. "That's 'cause I kicked my husband out. If you need to borrow a saddle today, I can lend you mine."

Marcy's measured response to what had seemed to me like a major drama was characteristic of the generous woman I would come to admire and of her horse's nature as well. Grouchy on the outside, Harley had the heart and loyalty of a golden retriever who weighs 1,400 pounds. The barn's mountaintop location overlooked a cluster of neighboring valleys and farms, nurturing my hopes for what I might accomplish in the spacious outdoor ring and the open fields behind the horse pasture where a massive elm tree stood. Even though I hadn't been at Pie Hill very long, I'd developed a nearly lyrical affection for that horse and his land, and I worried what my place was now that Alfonso was gone.

I worried for naught. Because her soon-to-be ex-husband had never been a fan of physical labor (or manure), Marcy had her hands full with barn chores and broken gates. She didn't have a lot of time for Harley, and said I'd be doing her a favor if I helped keep him in shape. She simply asked that I cover Harley's feed and always wear my helmet. I could even use her tack.

This opportunity was a supersized version of serendipity and a show of faith from the kind of woman who opts to trust people until she has a reason not to. The only problem was that Harley didn't seem to like me. For a horse-mad woman like myself who fantasized about a horse that came galloping and whinnying when I so much as whistled, Harley's standoffishness was dispiriting. It wasn't that he wasn't affectionate, per se, because he could be accommodating if you brought him a nice treat, it was just that he didn't want for much, so whenever I wanted to ride him, it was ultimately an interruption of his preferred pastimes of hay eating and sleep.

It turned out that Harley's detachment was exactly what my ego needed. Day after day, when I made it to the barn, I was confronted with a being who just wanted to *be*. Horses—or at least this horse—aren't susceptible to the desperate yearnings that torment human minds. Harley was comfortable in his Harley-ness, with little interest in whatever else I wanted him to be.

Since the polo mallets and the polo tack had disappeared with Alfonso, I concentrated on getting to know Harley and riding him correctly. After a few days together, I'd identified what appeared to be his only vices: he wouldn't stand still while you mounted him, and he had a canter that was more hold-on-for-dear-life than tallyho. In addition to hay and horse feed, Harley's great love was the red-and-white-striped peppermints I started buying by the pound, and in terms of fear, he was deathly scared of cat urine (I knew this because the neighbor's cat kept coming around to mark what he mistook as his territory) and storm drains. As someone riddled with my own fears, I respected his. I buried the house cat's urine under dirt and exhaled as I walked Harley past those pissy spots. I didn't avoid taking Harley out on the trails, but I talked to him and petted his big neck until the drain was far behind.

There wasn't a trainer at Pie Hill and I couldn't afford the added cost to truck one of my former instructors out, so I had to DIY my riding time with Harley. I was the only non-boarder at the stable, and the other women—when I crossed their paths at all—were polite but hurried: they weren't there to socialize, they were there to tack and ride. Thankfully, there was one boarder, a woman as lean as an asparagus in her late fifties name Michelle, who spoke up when she saw me making an amateur mistake.

"You've got the girth facing the wrong way—that little D ring there is in case you need to attach a training aid."

"This isn't how you put away a longe line—you've got to wrap it around your elbow and cinch it around the middle, here, or else it gets all tangled when you try to longe your horse."

"Don't get on him if he's walking away from the mounting block. Use your whip and guide him back to the mount, gently. You've got to train him out of it, not adapt to his bad habits."

I had no idea what kind of training aids could need attaching to a D ring, and my first attempt at longeing had ended with my horse facing me dead on and dumbly blinking, neither of us sure what the other one desired. But the whip thing worked. Using the far end of it and tapping him lightly in the direction that I wanted, I got Harley to stand still at the block.

Clarity, efficiency, and buckets full of patience, this was what Harley showed me lay between "desire" and "result." Clarity was not dinkling on my cell phone while my daughter asked to show me the double somersault she'd learned. Efficiency wasn't putting dried-out lime in tap water because a celebrity influencer claimed that it would stimulate my lymph nodes. Patience was about seeing the big picture and understanding that, yes, even though I had seen my daughter's attempt at a cartwheel seventeen times since Tuesday, she needed to know that her mother would choose watching her an eighteenth time over checking Twitter.

I started making a concerted effort to put away my phone until Nina was asleep. After moving the bulky collagen drink powder to yet another location in the kitchen, I finally said "Yes!" when Leo asked if he could throw the damn stuff out. Noticing that my facial lines became less jagged after a decent night's sleep (especially if that night had not involved red wine), I canceled my appointment with the injectables specialist and started blocking the Botox pushers that HTTP cookies had sent my way on Instagram. This was it: my face, my body, the shame inside my heart, and the things that I was proud of, this was what I had inside my toolbox at age thirty-eight, and botulism wasn't going to modify any part of my before.

Once my daughter was asleep and Leo was in his office facing off against the balance sheets and to-do lists and conference calls of a film in development, I'd sink into my latest rabbit hole online. My search-term history had shifted from "What do I do about nasolabial folds?" to "How can I tell if my horse likes me?"

"If you like yourself, your horse will too," responded exactly zero my search results. But it was true. When I walked out to Harley's pasture with a positive feeling in my belly, that today wouldn't be so much about me having a good riding experience as us growing our connection, Harley greeted me with his ears perked forward and his eyes alive and keen. On the flip side, when I stalked out to his pasture certain that our ride would result in another helter-skelter canter that would imperil anyone who dared to be in the ring at the same time, his eyes narrowed, his lovely mouth stayed closed, and his ears twitched back and forth, as unconvinced about the whole riding thing as I was.

Like a lot of humans, horses are sensitive, and they don't trust easily. The equine therapy trainer Cheyenne Price, who works predominantly with veterans struggling with PTSD, says that one of the reasons horses pair so well with people is that horses have no shame. "They don't have any fear of hurting anyone's feelings," she explains in a documentary called *The War Comes*

Home. "So if they don't like what's being put out on the table, they're gonna tell you."

My wants, my needs, my best-laid plans, they didn't mean jack shoot to Harley. Although parenting proved that I had to stay flexible to thrive (anyone who has experienced a blowout diaper while in transit can attest that this is true), I thought that flexibility was needed only up until a point. Once my daughter was out of the infant stage, I felt resentful and somewhat outraged by the nimbleness that mothering still demanded from me. And so Nina and I would fight. Fight about her footwear, fight about her bloody murder screams when I tried to wash her hair, fight about the fact that for no good reason, she refused to try red foods. Nina was a rock, and I was a rock, and I didn't see it as "good parenting" to turn into the water that flowed around the rock, so neither of us won, and nothing good or helpful came out on either side. But with horses, if you engender such a standoff, you don't get to ride. My desire to ride Harley was stronger than my unwillingness to compromise and be flexible, and so I started to learn what giving a little, and taking a little, actually looked like.

•

October turned to November: Nina brought home flyers about mitten trees and sock drives, penned her own letters to Santa in her giant, hard-won scrawl about how much she wanted a "unicorn light" that Leo and I stayed up scouring the internet to find. There had been more school shootings. All the headlines had the word "Trump" in them. My anxiety, which had been a muffled drumbeat, had been plugged into an amplifier. Autumn is simply a more colorful version of winter in our corner of Connecticut, a mealy mash of a season that is challenging to get through. Night falls at 4:30 PM, my work-from-home husband and I eat every single meal, take every single work call, parent, create, doubt, depress, and try to love each other out of the unchanging environment of a home usually buried in early snow. Despite the gloomy conditions, I knew I was making progress with my emotional and mental health. I saw it in the way my sleep had improved, and in my more regular breathing. I was putting weight on, slowly; my jaw felt less tense. But the seas of panic were rising nevertheless. Misogynistic rhetoric was everywhere, mass shootings were mounting, the right wing had returned its sights to the dismantling of *Roe v. Wade.*

When I felt dread closing in on me, I would shut my eyes and think of Harley: conjure the way his cheek smelled like hay dried in the sunshine, the soft white and rose and copper of his ever-changing roan coat. With no opportunities for coaching, I pushed polo out of my mind. For now, you ride, you get better, that's all that you can do, was what I'd say to myself when I started thinking back to how it felt on that black mare in the sand arena while the sun was rising, Victor shouting "*¡Vale, vale!*" at my side.

When Paugussett closed, I'd used the USPA's club locator to scout clubs near my house, but it came back spouting the names of faraway colleges I hadn't attended. I'd almost forgotten that I'd left a message on the machine of a privately owned club an hour from my house until I got a phone call in early November. Having intimate knowledge of what a barn office actually looks like, I had little confidence that someone would ever dust off the ancient machine I'd left a message on to call me back. But someone did.

"This is Alison Patricelli from Simsbury Polo?" the caller said. Alison apologized for taking so long to return my message—she'd been playing polo in Aiken, South Carolina, all fall, but she was back now, and the polo program she ran out of her barn, called Folly Farm, was about to open up again. Did I want to go out there and have a trial lesson so she could evaluate where I was at?

Derived from the French word for madness, in architecture, a "folly" refers to a generally expensive and indulgent whim that serves no purpose beyond the aesthetic. Gilded roof ornaments, pineapple-shaped pavilions, or in the case of Simsbury, Connecticut, the 165-foot Heublein Tower built into the bedrock of an imposing mountain ridge that runs behind the polo club. I hung up the phone with an initial lesson scheduled, feeling the folly of transcendence, very much indeed.

22

SASSY

Somewhere in Alabama, a pinto mare is being ridden badly by an on again, off again chief justice named Roy Moore. Roy Moore, a wealthy white man, is a far-right politician who believes that men should be the decision makers regarding what female bodies get to do inside and outside of their female skin.

And this goes for horses too. Moore owns a Tennessee walker mare that he calls Sassy. This is a man whose reputation for loitering at high school cheerleading practices and trolling local malls to solicit teenage girls predated—and accompanied—his rise to political power. That someone rumored to have a thing for underage women would name a female horse "Sassy" is galling enough, but that he would stuff a Tom Thumb bit inside her mouth, a bit designed for increased leverage action whose jointed middle slams into the roof of a horse's mouth when too much force is used, and ride this mare to vote for himself at the polls is so outrageous, one can only imagine the things that "Sassy" would say about this man if she could talk.

Except she can. Men like Roy Moore are so used to people keeping secrets for them that they forget that the mistreated have voices. Mares, too. In the videos that surface of Moore riding his poor horse to his local poll station, it's clear the mare is giving her rider every cue in her power to let him know that she is frightened and uncomfortable (her ears are pinned back, she's jumping sideways, her eyes are rolling upward), but instead of removing her from a distressing situation (or not forcing her into one in the first place), Moore starts hauling on her mouth, punishing her repeatedly for her public "nos."

The fall of 2016 wasn't a good time for women who were speaking up, and it was an even worse one for those already silenced. With my period still missing months past my miscarriage, I felt confused and overwhelmed by my own body, further frustrated by the fact that the medical professionals I had to talk to about that body were all male. I'd tried the only female doctor at Dr. Habert's obstetrics practice, but she insisted on calling my second-term dilation and curettage "an abortion." "That's just how we refer to it," she said, when I told her it was erroneous and the term upset me. In June, I had filed a letter of complaint against the anesthesiologist who had told me to "just make another one" when I cried over my lost pregnancy. Dr. Habert had called me about this letter, and listened while I cataloged his colleague's insensitivities, and that listening was one of the reasons I started seeing Dr. Habert again, and also one of the reasons I was disappointed when he wrote off my missing menses as early menopause, without understanding how that diagnosis—for a woman not yet forty—would land.

Men saying things clumsily, men speaking when they should have used their ears—that fall was a season of dry leaves and indignation. Encased in an unruly female body that had mothered a female, I was tempted to hate all men, to write their gender off, to send them all to Jupiter where they could get more stupider, but misandry wasn't going to help my anxiety or insomnia, wouldn't ensure my daughter's safety or my own or anyone else's, wouldn't protect us from the shootings that were on the rise again. A blanket hatred of men wasn't going to do anything but increase my cortisol levels and gray my hair and keep my lined face lined, tear the connective tissue in my marriage that had just begun to bind.

Nor was it going to help me to learn polo, the writing off of men. Polo is a coed sport, one of the few mixed-sex contact sports in rotation for somebody my age. With that being said, at the upper levels of polo, the people preparing the horses to be ridden, the people riding the horses, and the people paying for the whole shebang to come together are usually men. This is changing, with female patrons such as Melissa Ganzi and Maureen Brennan and my own coach, Alison, entering the heavily male mix, but the glass ceiling is just as high and hard to shatter in polo as it is in other realms. While I had no idea who was on the arena polo team that I was joining—Alison had mentioned a dentist, but she'd also mentioned a middle schooler—I was the rookie, the person joining them. Male, female, gender-fluid, it didn't matter, I had to learn from someone, and writing off an entire gender wasn't going to help me get the ball.

On the hour-long drive out to Simsbury for my first arena practice, my teammate concerns were replaced by apprehension around the fact that I was going to try and play at all. By the time the club's pastures came into sight, flanked on one side by an imposing mountain ridge, I was speculating about the speed that we'd be playing at. Fast, I hadn't done yet. Fast had me concerned.

•

With my bulky show hat under one arm and a battered water bottle in hand, I opened the door to the polo barn and found myself at one end of a seemingly mile-long aisle where the school horses were stalled. Up and down the barn aisle, people were focused on their grooming, ferrying out polo wraps and tendon boots and saddle pads and saddles to their waiting mounts. I stood there and swallowed, not sure of my next move, when suddenly I heard a lively, "Hey, you!" from the other end of the aisle. Coach Alison came to greet me with a smile and a high five, far more confident than I was about my presence in her barn. As an athlete, she probably believed in the upward trajectory of physical progress: that you improved as you learned, got better every time. But what if I played worse in this arena game than I had in the two lessons that I'd had with her? The stakes were so much different. What if I did something stupid, and somebody got hurt?

"Let me introduce you to everyone," said Alison, either not registering my growing disquiet or deciding to ignore it. She stopped at a stall where a petite girl was ministering to a beautiful white pony. "This is one of our star riders, Lizzie, and this is perfect Popcorn!" I stared in wonder at the two creatures, the tiny preteen blushing at Alison's compliment, and the dreamboat of a pony that she was brushing down. Lizzie was twelve years old, and had been show jumping until she made the switch to polo. Alison explained all this to me as we continued up the aisle. Lizzie was so shy that I didn't actually hear what her voice sounded like for weeks.

"And this is Clark," Alison said, moving ahead to the next stall, where a gangly teenager was struggling with an enormous bay who wasn't big on grooming.

"Hello," Clark said matter-of-factly.

We moved on to the next stall. "Jared, you've got your hoof pick on the ground, and your wraps have fallen in the horse bedding. Look alive, buddy, okay?"

Jared was a fifteen-year-old who was decidedly more garrulous than his compatriots, so much so that he tended to lose track of the task at hand in order to give himself completely to the discussion of whatever topic was preoccupying him that day: US-China trade wars, the commodification of privacy on the dark web, the future of robotics. Both he and Clark were in the gifted programs of their respective high schools.

Next up was Andrew, a college-age lad with movie-star good looks and the been-there-done-that air of someone who had much more exciting things to do than horse around with us. Andrew also came from the show-jumping world, but he was spending that season as a working student at Folly Farm, exercising and grooming the polo ponies that we'd be riding on. Aside from Alison herself and a sixty-something-year-old named Bruce who was nearing retirement from his dental practice, I was the only adult there. I did not feel like one, however. My nerves had my palms sweating and my armpits pricking with heat. During our kickoff chalk talk (which involved neither chalk nor a chalkboard, but rather Alison on her hands and knees behind two teams of plastic Breyer horses in the arena viewing room), I tried to concentrate on what Alison was saying about the toy horses meant to represent our positions in the arena, but my heartbeat was too loud.

"Now, you can ride somebody off here," Alison said, pushing the horse in the number one position right up against his equine defender, "but you have to meet shoulder to shoulder. Then you push and you push and you *push* the other player off the line. But you can't board them." Alison looked up, clocking our puzzled faces. She switched the position of the horses: the plastic horse on the left was now pushed up against the one on the right. "Let's say that the arena wall is to the right, here. You can't shove somebody up against it with your horse. That's called 'boarding,' and it's dangerous for the horses and dangerous for you. I see you putting my horses in danger, you'll be on the ground."

Given this information, the safest thing I could do was to stay still in the arena. Or drive home. That was an option too.

I looked at the huddle of players, trying to gauge everybody's familiarity with these rules and moves. In our first two lessons, Alison had run through the basic game for me: grass polo consists of four mounted players on each team playing through seven-and-a-half-minute time segments known as "chukkers." In grass polo, where the players actually change horses many times throughout the game to keep their horses fresh, there are usually between four and six chukkers and a halftime. In competitive arena polo, the smaller playing surface means there's only room for six players total, with the game lasting four chukkers. While arena players at the higher levels do switch out their mounts to avoid injuring or exhausting them, at our bush league level, we'd stay on the same horse the entire time, pause frequently for "teaching moments" and play for two chukkers before breaking to practice penalty shots and equitation.

In both arena and grass polo, there aren't any subs and nobody is benched: the team is the team, and if someone is injured, the players can enlist an emergency substitute—often a groom—but the substitute has to have the same or lower handicap as the injured player to keep the competing teams equal. Teams are demarcated by jerseys with the numbers one, two, three, and four on them (stopping at three in the arena), with number one being offense and number four being the defensive stronghold. The number three position is the equivalent of the quarterback in American football and is usually given to the strongest and most versatile player. In the arena, teams line up in descending order with player one on team A standing next to player three on team B and straight on down the line: this arrangement is known as "the train" and it's the way you're supposed to travel around the arena, with one player behind the other, man on man.

Regardless of whether you are right-handed or left-handed, the polo mallet is always held in the right hand, with the double reins clutched in the left. Everything that happens on the right side of your horse takes place on "the offside." Action to your left is on "the nearside." When you need to play on the left side of your horse, you don't put the mallet into your left hand; you say a Hail Mary, twist over your horse, and play with your right hand on the left side of your horse's neck. At a freaking gallop.

These basic rules made sense in my head when Alison was explaining them as I clopped after the ball in our private lessons, but now that I was encircled by the smells and pulses of these other players, the rules went from being abstract concepts to things that I was probably going to do badly and in an unsafe way.

"The most important thing," Alison said loudly, her voice pulling my attention back to our chalk talk, "is the line of the ball. In both grass and arena, there is an invisible line of fire that the train has to stay behind. You really have to think of the ball's trajectory as a line of fire. You cross the line, you get burned. I don't want you hurt, and I don't want you hurting my horses. Got it?" All the players offered their own version of a "yes." Mine was particularly adamant.

"Let's run through the defensive moves, then," Alison said, picking a dun-colored pony out from the Breyer pack to demonstrate the harrowing range of options on the defense menu. "We've talked about the ride-off," Alison reminded, pressing the dun pony up against a much larger stallion. "If you're successful at the ride-off—meaning, for example, that you have pushed your opponent to your right, and the ball ends up on your left—what is your play on the ball?"

"Nearside," said Clark, surely incorrectly, because that would mean twisting over your galloping horse to play a left side ball with your right hand.

"Yes! And if you don't take the nearside?"

"You cross the line of the ball," Clark said.

What was the line of the ball again? Where exactly was it? I winced at the herd of Breyer horses. Perhaps I could ride them?

"Perfect!" said Alison, clapping her hands together. "You guys got it. Let's play!"

It was time to get our steeds. In both of my lessons with Alison (the first had been an evaluation to comprehend my skill set, the second was for fine-tuning), I'd ridden a lovely pony named Estrella that Alison promised I could ride again in the arena. This prospect had initially boosted my confidence because I believed that the sturdy, clever Estrella had my best interests at heart. After all, I hadn't been run away with during my lessons, even though one of them had taken place outside in an area with no fencing on an unseasonably warm day. But as I walked toward the stall where the little black horse was waiting, I found a decidedly perkier Estrella than the one that I had known in my hour-long lessons. It turns out that horses, just like humans, know the difference between practice and game day.

I led Estrella into the arena, where my first realization was that the playing surface was very, very large, and the air cold enough to make the horses nervy. In the dairy barn where I'd first lessoned with Alison, I'd been held in a circular embrace the size of two tennis courts, but the indoor arena was football-field-sized with a ceiling three stories high. A girl could get run away with in here, I thought, as I made my way to the mounting block where I'd leave the ground behind.

From her horse, Argy, Alison organized us into teams: I was put on team B with Clark and Lizzie against Jared, Alison, and Bruce. My entire being yearned for another chalk talk, a few spontaneous life lessons shared from Alison's four-legged pulpit, maybe even a lightning bolt to cut the game short, but nothing came to stop our progress. I trotted after Lizzie and Clark to one side of the arena, where I was informed that Clark was going to "knock the ball in." The other players positioned themselves at various points to go after the ball wherever Clark hit it. And then Alison blew the whistle, and I felt it, the very rearrangement of the cells in Estrella's bloodstream: the mare was ready to play. Oh my God, I thought, she's going to gallop after the ball and I've barely even cantered. My own body was run through with the numbing swell of buyer's remorse: What in the hell was I doing there?

FWEET!! I was so stunned by the game's beginning that it took me several moments to realize that a whistle had been blown. "Courtney for obstruction! Jared's team gets a knock-in from the point of the foul."

I blinked into the space where the whistle's noise had been. Huh? What foul? Obstructing what? Estrella pulled and strained against me, eager to move her little body as I tried to piece everything together. "You can't stand still in polo," Alison shouted. "You'll block the train. It's dangerous. You have to *move.*"

BAM! Jared slammed the ball in the direction of his goal— dear God, it almost hit us. I jerked Estrella out of the way and she pulled her head the opposite direction in protest of my roughness with her mouth. For no reason that I could see, everyone was cantering to the opposite goal.

"We change directions after every goal!" Alison called back from the stampede.

What the hell am I doing here, what the hell am I doing here, went my rabbit heart.

•

Although I take emotional risks as a writer, I am not a physical risk taker. I bring my daughter sledding in the winter but beg off from the actual sledding part because even modest hills give me butterflies. We have a log stretching over a small stream in our backyard that runs between our property and a friend's house, and although Nina runs back and forth across that thing in a princess dress and light-up slippers, it's all I can do not to get down on my bottom and scuttle across it when it's wet.

When we are children, especially if we have supportive and energetic caretakers, we are encouraged to try things until we find what sticks. But as we enter adulthood, many of us—myself included—cling safely to what works. When we find the career that seems right for us, we work to rise up in that career. When we form our circle of friends, we deepen the relationships within that specific circle, and for those of us who are monogamous, we do what it takes to turn one of the many people in our universe into the everlasting "one."

What is a midlife crisis other than a widening of these circles, a breaking of such patterns? A rising up against the order we have established, a sudden yearning to be great, or at least knowledgeable, in something that we haven't been doing very much of? "She dropped her legal practice to become an herbalist," "He divorced his wife for a woman twenty years his senior," "She finally came out." We've all heard the stories of the people who up and left the life that they were "good" at for something that "came out of nowhere," a passion speeding across their psyche like a blazing comet.

But these rebellions don't come out of nowhere. When we bang our fists against the bars of middle age, it's usually because there is a voice within us that is sick to death of going unused. I was wrong about my mother's motorcycle. It hadn't been something that she'd "picked up" after a divorce she hadn't wanted. I called my mom to ask her about it, to match up what I remembered with what I was writing, and she said she had been a motorcycle enthusiast in her youth. She had had a boyfriend, one of her last loves before she married my father, who used to take her everywhere on his Harley-Davidson. The boyfriend had given her lessons, but she'd never had the courage to try motorcycling herself, until the divorce opened up a door for her that she could now go through. The Sportster that I remembered coming out of nowhere didn't come out of nowhere. And this is true—stays true—even if the Sportster didn't stay.

While horseback riding was in the general—if distant—range of my abilities, polo playing wasn't. After that first arena match, I stood downtrodden in the stall with Estrella, taking off her saddle blanket and her saddle with a heavy heart because I had been slower and clumsier and more afraid than I'd expected. Polo was too complicated and too fast and too dangerous; I was a fool and a waster of numerous people's time to have heeded what I'd mistaken as a calling to the sport.

I bent down to unwind the dirtied polo wraps from Estrella's legs, listening to the voices of my teammates calling out for towels and curry combs for their far sweatier horses. Estrella side-eyed me: *You were better than this in lessons.*

I know, I replied, undoing the braid in her pinned-up tail, *I'm sorry. I won't bother you again.*

Estrella exhaled in a great puff. Happy? Disappointed? I looked up, and her ears were forward. *You give up too easily,* she seemed to say. *And that's the most disappointing thing yet.*

23

THE SECRET PLACE

In the house that I grew up in when my parents were still married, there was a crop of spotted laurel underneath an oak tree, in the middle of which lay a rock that had the power to grant invisibility.

That rock was a happy place for me: I accepted its superpowers when I had trying but exciting things to do inside the woods behind my home, like hunt for robin redbreasts, the messengers of the unicorns I was sure lived back there too. The outdoors was a place that fueled all the magic and the madness and the mystery of my mind.

There was an evergreen tree on the outskirts of my parents' property that was my favorite sentry—the one I chose from all the giants there. This particular evergreen was spindly and sap-filled, forever leaving sticky goops on my school kilt that were impossible to get out, deposits that attracted lint and feathers and whatever else they touched. But I loved that little tree above all others, and a special ritual of mine was to take my favorite

Christmas tree ornament from any given year and "liberate" it by hanging it on the highest branch of my outdoor tree, where it would keep watch over the house and, accordingly, me. When I learned that our house was going to be sold, and a moving date was set, I climbed up that tree with my all-time favorite ornament, a life-sized cardinal with real feathers, and set him up there on that branch, for life.

When I came back to the East Coast early, before Leo joined me from Paris to start the American chapter of our lives, I made the drive out to the Tudor home that I had lived in as a child. The bordering evergreens were still there, bushy with pine needles, but so much smaller than I'd kept them in my mind: although I'd thought myself unseeable during my tree climbs, I must have been visible to anyone who walked by. Was the ornament still there? It would have required a certain level of trespassing to find out—I would have had to breach the property, and if not *scale* it, exactly, I would have had to sidle up to that tree's trunk. Whether the bird was still there mattered less, I decided, than the fact that the house and property were, a stretch of land that had fed my imagination for so many years, had taught me how to carve out pockets of magic where I could feel fierce and safe.

As an adult nearing forty, my secret places were gone. Even my physical whereabouts were common knowledge to the smartphone I had to keep on in case there was a problem with our daughter at school. Marriage had boarded up the rooms of romance and flirtation I used to escape to as a younger woman, but I'd been convinced that I could rekindle some of that excitement in the sport of polo. But my being bad at polo, or rather, my unwillingness to risk being decent by going fast, was complicating my access to that underworld, and with it, the thrill of having my own secret life again.

When I drove home after my first arena match at the new club, I shut down Leo's inquiry into how the game had gone with a muttered, "I need to think about it." I'd wanted to come home and say that the various times he'd stayed home with Nina so I could meet this man or that woman for a lesson, the times I'd been laser-focused on some horse video with him next to me, wanting to chitchat on the couch, were all worth it, because it turned out that I had a gift for the sport of kings. But this wasn't the reality. *I spent the evening terrified, I felt the fool, I couldn't canter* wasn't going to cut the mustard, so I kept my reflections to myself. It would all end now, anyway, so what use was it sharing what an underperformer I had been? I imagined I would wake the next day with my tail between my legs and call Alison—maybe chicken out and text her—to say I wasn't cut out for that next level of play, that I was grateful for the lessons and wished the team the best. But I woke up the next day with that magnet pull, instead. Pulled toward something that I wasn't good at, that made me afraid. When the group text came through midweek, assembling the teams that coming Monday, Alison wrote, "Who's in?" with a strong-arm emoji. Against the protests of my left brain, I said that I would play.

24

THE YEAR OF THE HORSE

I was born in September 1978, so my Chinese birth year is the year of the horse. Given what a noble and powerful creature the horse is widely accepted to be, one might assume that people born under this birth sign are noble and confident, too. But we horses are the most insecure of breeds.

When I started riding again, I unearthed a battered guidebook to my Chinese birth year on eBay. Despite the fact that the book was published in 1982, reading it nevertheless felt like my critical superego was delivering a performance review to my freewheeling id. In a section called "A few notes on the Horse," I found:

PRINCIPAL DEFECTS: Unstable, flares up easily, impatient and talkative.
WORK: Ambitious and hates to lose.
CANNOT LIVE WITHOUT: Being supported, encouraged, complimented or even applauded.
FAVOURITE PLACES: Everywhere, other than where he lives. Often prefers the homes of others. He hates to be hemmed in.

The book told me that the horse year had four ages: both my child-hood and youth would be difficult ones in which I'd be forced into self-reliance on the emotional and fiscal fronts, and would have, on numerous occasions, to "sell out" to survive. In the maturity stage, I was sure to find "calm and equilibrium" because I would have learned "the wisdom of failure and the value of perseverance." Old age for us horse types would be docile and serene.

On the professional front, I had, in fact, persevered. With the horse contact helping me regulate my blood pressure and stress levels, I'd been sleeping better, and made it to my work desk each day with a clearer mind. That mind was far better equipped to finish the book I'd originally promised to my editor—which concerned the impact of social media on mental health—and to chuck out the dressage champion and horse-breeding characters who had no place in that novel other than to signal to my heart and brain that I wanted horses back.

With church and state finally separated, I turned my second novel in, and a publication date was set. In many ways, I was still tethered to my publisher: there were months ahead of mar-keting talk and publicity strategizing, the designing of a cover, the seeking out of blurbs, the hope against hope that the book would publish in a receptive climate and that the press would be kind. All this, the business side of publishing, was a gauntlet that I wasn't through yet, and I would run through that gaunt-let carefully: that novel had been hard for me to get right, my publisher had been patient, and I wanted it to do well. But in the bigger, vaster picture, I was a free agent. I had had one novel under contract, and I'd just turned that book in. Though my editor was eager to continue working with me and I liked her a great deal, there was something I craved more than professional security, which was the taking back of my creative instincts to my magic rock. I wanted to make things without anybody looking at my secret heart.

"Do you have any idea of what you want to do next?" my literary agent asked me, a few weeks after I'd turned my book in.

"I need to be left alone for a while," I said. "I need to do my thing."

My agent has always been a good reader of energy. She did what I asked and left me alone: I was free to soar or falter as I saw fit, but I would be doing so without the safety net of a book advance. This freedom, if frightening, was nonetheless thrilling, and it coincided with my making very little progress on the polo field.

I've always been spatially challenged with a disastrous sense of direction, and exhibit an impairment called "dyscalculia" in all things math-related. Unfortunately for me, polo is about angles. Arena polo rules stipulate that players need to meet the ball "fairly" at all times, which means that you can't go charging toward another player at a ninety-degree angle just because you see the ball emerge out of a herd of horse legs. But I didn't know what a ninety-degree angle looked like at a canter, and I was so stuck on trying to figure out my angle of approach that I lost track of where the ball was.

"Foul on Courtney! Obstruction! Other team knocks in!"

"Dangerous riding!"

"High hook!"

"Other team knocks in!"

As part of her safety-first coaching style, Alison could go from being my biggest advocate to being my harshest critic in the seconds it took me to do something dumb. Was it possible that I was this daft, this clumsy, this incompetent, or did she just have it out for me?

"Dead ball!"

"Boarding!"

"Other team knocks in!"

I wasn't on Estrella in my second practice—I was downgraded to a prehistoric, placid mare called Mimosa that belonged to Alison's young son. Mimosa had basically two gaits, the slow walk and the fast trot. But despite this mare's lack of speed and her utter dependability, I still managed to muck up every shot, which made my eyes prick with shame. I was in a hell of my own making, mystified and stunned. I couldn't see what I was doing wrong. The play was too fast, the angles too confusing. I felt like I was free-diving next to people with oxygen tanks on. Lizzie was only twelve years old, dammit—and was speeding up and down the arena making not a foul. Jared was moving so quickly I couldn't even see what he was doing, but I could hear him hit the ball. And me? I was getting in people's way and making the whistle toot. I wondered if everyone resented me like I resented myself.

"A Horse may be regarded as intelligent and be respected in his profession," my astrology book said, but:

> he will navigate continuously between two extremes, at times announcing enthusiastically that he will get the better of everyone because he is the best; at others, doubts and self-destructive feelings will convince him that he is good for nothing. Yet at such times he will have the secret hope that someone will come to reassure him, whereupon he will start out again, passionate and frisky.

"Get your head back in the game, C.!" I swiveled to the right, astonished. This advice had come from Lizzie. I edged forward in my saddle, certain I hadn't heard her correctly: Lizzie turned beet red whenever I tried to talk to her while we were tacking up, question her about school, how she had come to riding. But it was Lizzie who had spoken. She smiled at me mischievously, then cantered away.

"What are you doing? GO!" Lizzie scream-whispered the next time she was parallel to me, before galloping off again.

The fact that Lizzie was talking to me after staying close-lipped for so long opened something inside of me. Though I felt like I was a disaster in the arena, I was nevertheless *there*, present and alive. I felt solid and visible, suddenly aware that even with my ineptitude, I was needed by my teammates.

"I don't know what I'm doing," I admitted to my new friend as we strode side by side on our first walk break. Lizzie's face reddened, but she managed a tight smile: apparently she was less loquacious at a walk than at the gallop.

"You just need to *play*," Lizzie insisted, as Alison blew the whistle to signal that the game was starting up again.

25

TEACHING IS LOVE

Concurrent with my tribulations in arena polo were my attempts at mental progress during my ongoing therapy sessions with Joe. As the 2016 calendar flipped to 2017, he focused on my obsession with productivity and success. Joe had a hunch that I used these as defense mechanisms, and he wanted to know why.

"When you were little how did you validate yourself?" Joe asked during one of our eucalyptus-scented sessions in his narrow office.

"Grades," I said without a moment's hesitation.

"And what about now?"

I answered that it was important to me that I keep writing and publishing books, that people see me as an active writer, that readers and editors like and respect the things I wrote.

"Okay," said Joe, "and when things don't go as planned, when someone doesn't like your book, or something you wrote fails. Who are your firefighters in these situations?"

I blinked at him, confused.

"Who are the people who help you put these fires out?"

That horrid throat tightening again.

"Let's back up," Joe said, seeing my emotions rise. "When you were a child, who were your firefighters then?"

I held back the waterworks. I tried to clear my throat. Joe took advantage of my silence to write four categories on the whiteboard: "Professional, Emotional, Romantic, Social." Who were my firefighters in these areas when I was younger?

I looked at each column. "Myself, myself, myself," I said, before dissolving into tears.

•

When I was little, it was not enough to be good at what I was good at; I had to be the best. Curiously, this pressure was never put on me by my parents: really, it was the opposite. With the exception of my grandmother and, later, my half sister on my father's side, no one in my family read. You'd sooner find a guava in my house than a dog-eared book. I wasn't pushed in any one direction as a child, was left to find my own path, so why did I push myself so hard when I found it?

For so long, unrelenting, steely-nerved perfectionism was my only coping mechanism as my brother's health faltered and my parents' marriage failed. To excel, to overachieve, to be productive, to be quick, this was what I drew my strength from, even if I sometimes had to cut corners—valuing style over clarity in my college essays, or reading an assignment too quickly to pick up on a text's nuance—to get there. In polo, however, I couldn't cut corners. I couldn't dazzle with my aptitude. I was anything but quick.

On the third arena match at Simsbury, I was going for the fearsome nearside—leaning out precipitously over the left side of my horse—when Jared swung at my mallet for a hook with too much force, hitting my poor horse in the head, which sent her rearing to the right, and me smashing to the ground. The fall hurt less than I had feared it would; the wind wasn't knocked out of me, nothing broke or was even sprained, and the horse was okay too. But it hurt my ego.

On the first walk break of that game, I sidled up to Lizzie. "I'm gonna quit if I fall off again," I dared.

This time, she spoke back to me in a normal voice. "You can't quit," she said. "You're part of the team now."

This was when I realized something revolutionary: out there in the arena, I was ensnarled in a psychological battle that no one else had noticed. That I wanted to be great at this quickly, that I wanted to be the best, this hadn't occurred to any of my teammates and would have seemed preposterous if it had. I was a beginner. A total beginner. Why was I being so tough on myself? No one else was making me play polo: I'd got myself there. So why wasn't I having fun? Laughing at the absurdity of it, an almost-forty-year-old learning to play polo alongside a natural who was twelve? A mother flat out on her back with a mound of poop near her right shoulder—why was that tumble proof of my incompetence and my unteachability, instead of what it had been: a fall? A fall, and nothing more.

Years out from that initial firefighter conversation with my therapist, I'm embarrassed by the answer that I gave him. It was ungenerous and disingenuous of me to claim that I had only myself to lean on in tough times. First of all, I had wonderful teachers—teachers who looked out for and second-parented me, who rooted for me and chastised me and tried, if not to save me, than at least to alert others to the darker urges of my worst self. I came upon a paragraph in a novel the other day that opened this realization to me, a new book by Sigrid Nunez, in which a dying friend is relating how much school meant to her as a child. "School, in general, made me feel loved," Nunez writes. "That somebody wanted to teach me things, that they cared about my penmanship, my stick-figure drawings, the rhymes in my poems. That was love. That was most surely love. . . . Teaching is love."

After my best friend Kristin, there was Rebecca, and after Rebecca, there were Nick and Josefina. Throughout my teenage years, I always had a best friend whose family I adored, and a steady boyfriend. Though my father was confusing in the way he showed it, both he and my mother loved me and wanted me to stay with them, literally stay with them, to be more visible, more present, but they didn't insist upon it, and so I drifted like a balloon released into the sky. As for my brother, he was ill and young, and I was too self-involved and scared of what was happening to him to imagine that it could be any other way than what it was: Brendan on a hospital bed, me on the other side of a viewing window, deciding there was nothing I could do for him, for us.

If I was alone at times and overly self-sufficient as a young person, that had often been my choice. There were firefighters all around me and there always had been. People who reached out and said, You're part of this team now, don't leave us.

26

HORSE TO WATER

The autumn I joined the team at Simsbury Polo, my mother and I had one of the biggest fights we'd had since the screaming matches of my teenage years. Her decision to vote for a presidential candidate who hated a lot of things, but women in particular, felt like a nail in the coffin of our already strained relationship. I warned that I would never think of her the same way if she cast her vote as she intended to, and that her relationship with her beloved granddaughter might also be altered. She cried that it was an infringement on her liberties, my trying to influence her vote. The fight went on, ending in slammed doors and sobs, and my mother's insistence that I take her to the airport and cut her visit short.

I did not take her to the airport and my mother didn't alter her voting plan, casting a ballot that fell in line with the voting patterns of my family tree. Recognizing that I had no right to withhold my daughter from the grandparents who adored her, but also feeling justified in my disappointment and rage, I turned to Joe to help me understand what kind of bridge I could build over my family's political differences going forward.

I look back now and have to laugh at the woman who assumed that the sporty man she'd met at her intake session was too young and immature to be her therapist. In the time we had been working together, Joe showed an understanding of human nature—and a willingness to forgive its baser urges—that stemmed far beyond his age. His challenge to me whenever I started railing about my parents was to constantly ask myself what had happened in their past that led them to their actions in the present, and whether I could think of our differences with compassion first.

His questions to me were profound but also straightforward, and I jotted them down like homework assignments while we talked.

"You wish your mother were different. But what can you respect about her?"

"What happens when you imagine your stepfather getting comfort out of watching Fox News?"

"How can you accept the people your parents have chosen to be?"

"Which is more possible: the likelihood of your parents changing, or them not knowing how to change?"

Of course, this model of acceptance needed to be extended to my husband and my daughter, because they sometimes did things that made them my enemy too.

"Leo's creative process is slower to cook than yours. What does that have to do with you?"

"Nina listens more to Leo than to you. In that listening, is she trying to say something about the way you speak to her?"

Joe's compassion-first approach even stretched to my insomnia: "Is it possible that your insomnia is trying to protect you in some way?"

If an abacus existed that totaled the caloric expenditure of one person trying to change another, my number would be high. For years, truly, years, I had worked to change the people closest to me, and resented them when they didn't change, instead of trying to change anything about myself. But the horses made me change.

There was not going to be a Hollywood-movie ending for me where a scrappy coach unearthed my potential and I soared into the elite realm of professional female polo players with the unheard-of handicap of ten. I was not gifted at polo, but I had enough motivation to get from "bad" to "better," and this was the first time in my life that I decided to stick with something I wasn't great at just because I liked it.

My recognition of my averageness and commitment to keep on playing polo despite it was a liberation. If my learning polo wasn't a means to a concrete end, then that meant I was doing it for fun, which meant—or at least implied—that I could have fun while doing it. If I could have fun while riding, maybe I could have fun while writing, too. And if these two things were possible, then it didn't seem impossible to try having fun with motherhood.

Little by little, I started to use the tools that Joe was giving me to view my daughter in a new way. Her decision to wear mismatched socks yanked high over the leggings she'd worn four days in a row was Nina asserting her own fashion sense. Placing four necklaces over the turtleneck that no longer fit her but reminded her of when she was a toddler was both a sartorial choice and a display of nostalgia. Here my daughter had been trying for months to show me what kind of person she was becoming, and I had chosen to see, instead, a little girl who was trying to make my mornings difficult. I stopped second-guessing Nina's fashion choices, stopped pleading with her to wear the leggings that were any pair but the ones she liked best. I let her dress the way she wanted to. I let her have her fun.

As Joe had taught me to, I turned next to my husband, intent on rediscovering who he was instead of who and what he wasn't. I had come to regard Leo as an earmuffed ship captain so intent on moving his vessel forward that he hadn't noticed I'd fallen off the boat. I had seen him this way for so long that I had become intellectually incapable of appreciating his qualities, and also the ways in which he'd been trying to throw me a life raft. Through Joe, I learned about the five different love languages, how some people show affection through gifts, others through attention, words, touch, or actions of service, and it was in learning about these communication styles that I realized Leo and I had been speaking different languages for years. I was a word person, waiting for Leo's words, but Leo was and always had been a person who showed his love in actions.

I thought back to the birthday present he'd given me the year before, a down mattress topper I had been miffed by because I assumed—as I had the year before that one, in which he gave me a digital camera though I rarely take photos—that the mattress topper was something that he wanted, but had given me instead, making it a gift for us. But knowing about the love languages, I suddenly saw these gifts differently. Leo had given me that mattress topper because he thought it might help with my insomnia.

It was just that he hadn't said this, because he wasn't a word guy, and thus, I had heard that he didn't love me. Even the gift of the digital camera, that had been an invitation into Leo's world, where images and colors reigned over similes and words. I was ashamed to think back on my indignation, how convinced I'd been that he was the weak link, when, in actuality, I simply hadn't seen the ways in which he was trying to help.

•

Meanwhile, there was a new addition to our motley polo family who was buttressing the "let it be" lessons I was learning in therapy with Joe. The polo club's working student, Andrew, decamped for the South and was replaced by an even-keeled Argentinean groom named Martin, whose fervent hollers of "¡Relájate!" while he tore up and down the arena echoed what I was learning on the home front.

Just relax. Sit back, have fun. Easier said than done when you're on a half-ton animal in a herd of other animals, but I started to get there.

After Mimosa, I was upgraded to a larger bay named Kat, an honest gelding who made up for the fact that he was hard to turn ("Plan early!" Alison would shout) with a buttery canter and a straight approach to every ball. Something odd came out of those Monday practices: I was terrible at grasping the big picture of the game, still a dunderhead with angles, but my swing was a secret weapon. Alison started saying that I had a natural swing, which I assumed was just her trying to assuage me for the myriad other things I had done wrong at every practice, until I started noticing—during penalty shots, especially—that my shots went fast and landed true.

This was something of a revelation: my upper arms were the width of a baguette, and the only muscle in my body then was probably my heart. My workout regimen during the week consisted of fast typing and hunting down Nina's beloved leggings from the laundry pile upstairs. I didn't have a lot of confidence in my riding—I leaned forward too much, didn't keep my weight in the right place, and hadn't quite figured out how to control a horse's speed with my legs instead of my hands—but I was starting to gain confidence in my polo swing. I wasn't good, but I was less terrible than I had been. I was making progress.

Between the preparations for my novel's publication, the ramping up of Leo's efforts to find the right person for his film's lead role, and the time spent encouraging Nina's newfound love of cartwheels and balance biking, it was a busy winter. Before I knew it, little buds were sprouting from the trees again, the snow slushed into puddles, and suddenly, it was spring. In early May I got a phone call from a number I didn't recognize.

"¡*Mamacita!*" the voice shouted when I answered. "We're back!"

I could not believe that Victor remembered the novice he'd given a polo lesson to back in late September, much less that he'd found a way to get in touch. I was dumbstruck on the other end of the telephone, so unsure as to why he'd be calling that I wondered if I'd left something at the barn all those months ago.

"You ride with us tomorrow?" he thundered.

My heart dropped.

"Seven AM?" he said. "We'll play!"

27

I LEARNED IT BY WATCHING YOU

I showed up at Paugussett with a litany of disclaimers ("I'm not much better than last time," "I'm scared of going fast," "I think I'm still at the point where the horse is riding me"), none of which I was able to use because Victor was more interested in introducing me to his horseman friends and relatives than he was in hearing how little I'd progressed.

"This is my nephew, Carlos," Victor said, throwing his arm around a smirking man with youthful skin and a flattop haircut. "He has learned everything from me, although he has learned nothing."

"Is that right?" Carlos responded, gripping his uncle's shoulder playfully. "Because I think it is the other way around!"

Next up I met Danny, the owner of a steering columns company who hailed not from the Dominican Republic but from a town in Westchester County that he commuted from every morning to exercise the horses and perform barn chores before starting his own work.

"Danny is our fouler," Victor said, pulling the much taller Danny close. "You must watch what he does, and then you never do it."

"I learned it by watching you!" said Danny, who also answered Victor's gibe with an affectionate squeeze. This was a group of tactile men, men who pinched and patted and slapped and hugged each other constantly. In the two minutes I'd been standing in the gaping entrance of the polo barn, they'd been more physical with each other than I usually was with my own husband. But Victor's barn wasn't made up of only men.

"And that is Leah," Victor called out, nodding in the direction of a young woman with long hair flowing untethered down her back. She was crouching over some kind of alfalfa mixture she was mashing for the horses, and looked up briefly with a flat "Hey." Leah's greeting, which was cooler and more distanced than those of the other grooms, made me wonder if my presence was a burden.

After the introductions were made and innuendos exchanged about the extent to which this man or that man was a better rider than the other, the men returned to whatever they'd been doing, carrying out the fetching and grooming of the horses without any indication as to what I was meant to do, myself. When Victor pointed at a black mare that Carlos had on one end of lead rope and said, "That's yours," I understood that the grooms were used to accommodating Victor's strays.

Carlos set about flinging one piece of tack after another over the wooden stall behind the horse that I would ride. I stared, intimidated, at the well-worn saddle blankets and sheepskin girths and double-reined bridles, wishing that I had something beneficial to offer this horse and this man.

"Can I help at all?" I asked, the inflection in my voice doing little to convince either of us that I could actually be of use.

"Oh yes, you can help me, certainly!" Carlos answered with the close-lipped smile that I would come to recognize as his trademark, as he tacked, in thirty seconds flat, the entire horse for me.

I knew from watching it happen at Simsbury that the fact that there were five horses saddled and three times that without any tack at all meant that we were going to pony the horses on the gallop track. Ponying horses is a way of saving time during morning exercises: by roping up horses to a mounted leader, a single rider can exercise up to six horses at a time.

The horse I was given to ride was named Pajita, a beautiful black mare who was fast if you asked for it, but well tempered most of the time. Leah told me that her name meant "little masturbation" in Argentinean slang, a moniker that did justice to her nimbleness, her satiny canter, and her manageable size.

I was given two horses to pony to the other riders' three or four, but that suited me just fine. Walking out to the gallop track as clusters of other riders exited their respective barns with the fog of dawn lifting and the sunshine burning through it, I felt so proud I thought I might burn right through my saddle. None of the grooms looked at me askance or seemed to doubt my riding ability. Clearly, when Victor decided that somebody got to ride with them, they all assumed the person could ride.

•

There have been a lot of joyful moments in my life, and I am fortunate for that. But riding around that gallop track in the early turn of morning remains among the happiest. Attached to the horsepower of several tremendous creatures through a cord of nylon rope, and guiding those hearts and muscles with the power of my legs, with the exception of giving birth and that one time I mustered the courage to swim in northern Maine, I'd never felt so alive.

Each barn at Paugussett had a cohort of three or more grooms ponying five horses, so although there were nearly forty horses on the track, each barn rode together, and the flow felt organized.

At Simsbury, Alison had taught us to put safety first and second, and so even though I was aware that there were a lot of safety precautions being breached out on the track—I was the only rider with a helmet on that morning, though regulations have since changed—I couldn't keep from thinking how devastatingly cool all the grooms were. Leah was beside me with her long hair flowing in cascades down her back, her simple tennis sneakers bulwarked by the polo wraps around her legs. Two grooms were in front of us talking on their cell phones, one of them while smoking. Another groom was ponying five horses *bareback*. The air was thick with a swagger that Leah and I cut through—judging by appearances, we were the only women on the track: an anomaly that would remain the case all summer.

The gallop track was gated on the right side. On the left, it was flanked by shrubbery and trees. Victor was ahead of us with the other grooms, and called back to us to trot. Looking around, I noticed that the other riders were barely posting—they weren't rising up and down dramatically as riders in most English disciplines do—so I followed their lead, or tried to, my spinal cord protesting with every bumpy attempt to be as suave as them. At this gait, some of the exercises' trickier aspects manifested themselves: the horse on my right wanted to go faster than the other two, and that horse's rope (a big, gnarly cord of fraying nylon) was burning my ungloved hand. We went around and around the track, my "*¡Buen día!*" to the passing riders more enthusiastic than Leah's, for whom ponying wasn't an exhilarating once-in-a-lifetime opportunity but a daily job. By the third pass around the track at a trot, my stomach muscles protested: my posture was terrible, unnatural, my shoulders either too slouched or arched prissily back. How did the other riders look so casual about this? Although I knew that this was familiar to them—as natural as an instinct—it didn't keep me from gawking at their ability. They made it all seem effortless, but like they were in control at the same time. Relaxed, practiced, and confident as hell.

"*¡Galope!*" Victor called. My stomach clenched at the meaning of this word, and the transition it represented. Leah moved into a canter the second Victor's command hit, and my horses followed suit while my confidence slipped into the dust behind us. A garbled noise escaped my throat, its tightness reminding me to breathe. How could I communicate to Leah that I didn't know what I was doing? It would be over the top, wouldn't it, to call out *Help?*

It turns out that when you've got subpar form, you don't need to utter anything: your mistakes are on display. Leah slowed her string so I could catch up with her, and with our horses mashed together at the canter, we moved around the ring, Leah exaggerating her own movements so that I could copy them. What impressed me—and was impressed upon me—was that her body wasn't this immobile structure; it was moving with the horses,

197

in response to them. In my prior lessons, it had been drummed into me, literally (one of my teachers had me ride with a whip rammed behind my back and held in the crooks of my elbows), to keep my posture straight, but the riders that passed us—Leah included—moved like people on top of a live animal, and they themselves, alive. That isn't to say that their shoulders were undisciplined or their cores collapsed, but rather that their riding was sensual and physical.

Danny and Carlos whistled as we circled around them for the third and then a fourth time, when my body was moving as it should. There have been times when I haven't welcomed catcalls, when they have made me feel tracked and vulnerable, but that day was no such time. Their attention made my heart swell; I wanted to cheer for the fact that after years spent living among the head-down foodies of the Berkshires, someone finally noticed me. And I didn't look half-bad! I'd put seven pounds on my frame since the worst months of my depression, and all the riding and grooming was strengthening my core.

Something became clear at the end of that bright morning: Carlos was showing me a special kindness, a favoritism. At first I thought I was imagining it—they were jokers, that mixed group of Dominicans and Americans, tossing provocations between each other in a season-long rally of insults and one-ups, so maybe this was just the way Carlos was. But that was not what it felt like. My nerves were on alert around him and blood rose to my face. This man, ten years my junior, was attracted to me, and my body was responding.

This was a revelation, as startling and unexpected as those rare times that you find someone else's money lying on the ground.

For so long, I had lived the structured but pleasant life of a free-lance writer in the woods. Working out of my home all day in some grubby outfit, sprucing myself up for drinks or food with other couples once in a while. With the exception of the annual writing conferences I attended or panels I occasionally sat on, I didn't meet new people save for the ones I invented in my fiction. I'd gone a long time feeling that physical isolation was the key to my productivity: no distractions, peace and quiet. But that morning at Paugussett, I realized that it had also contributed to my depression. At thirty-eight, with my menses AWOL, I felt unfeminine and invisible, a cardboard cutout Courtney among my family and friends. The men and women in our social circle were determined graphic designers and acupuncturists whose free time was spent babysitting sourdough starters, hand-roasting coffee beans, and pulling ramps from mud. The menfolk were good fathers and focused husbands, but they were earnest, not flirtatious. And while it was, let's say, edifying to be among steadfast people, I was positively desperate for lust. In my twenties when I lived in France, I'd been a club goer, a party thrower, a party attendee: from Thursday through the weekend, my body was usually pressed against another's in some thrumming crush. In the city—or at least in Paris—I was constantly reminded that I lived inside a body that other people noticed. In the hipster countryside, I had a body that did not rock climb or plant shrubs.

But horseback riding—and polo in particular—demanded that I shake things up. Where I'd gone soft and hunchy, riding needed me strong. No more sleepy calves and lethargic legs—I needed lengthened muscles to keep my heels down in the stirrups for impressively long goes. Legs to belly, bridle over head, a hoof full of manure cradled in a hand: I was back inside the world of touch.

28

OPERATION SAVE THE WHODATT FUR BABIES

Who adopts a cat they've never met? I asked myself on the two-hour drive out to Yonkers, New York, where the cat I'd adopted off a hope, a prayer, and a couple Facebook photos was waiting for me.

It had been five years since our beloved Maine coon cat, Mylo, had died—at only seven years old, he'd suffered a blood clot that paralyzed him from the waist down. He couldn't urinate, couldn't walk—we had to euthanize him a month before our daughter's birth. I'd been ready for a while for another pet, but Leo—who had been Mylo's confidant and bestie—hadn't been. As for Nina, she had weathered the news that we had lost my second pregnancy with the self-interest of a preschooler: she had wanted a sister anyway, so we had to make her a sister right away. She'd been on me all the time about her sibling needs that winter, even going so far as to say "it" could be a brother if it absolutely had to be, or an older sister. Just a sibling, any kind would do.

Though Nina didn't mean the fur kind of sibling, a pet was where we landed. After the miscarriage, both Leo and I agreed that sticking with an only child was the best way to keep our marriage and our sanity intact. It was my idea to gift Nina with a cat. If she was going to be an only child, it seemed only right that she should have a furry pet.

I'd spent the spring researching animals. It hadn't been hard to find Mylo, so I never imagined that the process would be different our second time around. Turns out that good shelters are wary of sending kittens to a home with a preschooler crouched in wait. I thought we'd be the perfect adoptive parents: we worked from home, were ever present, the cat would rarely be alone. But I couldn't get anybody to return my calls. It seemed that checking the "child in the house" box was the death knell for our eligibility as cat parents.

I moved away from our A-list choices to B and C. When I got to D (Leo wanted a kitten, but kitten season had passed), I finally got a call back. My phone's screen flashed a Louisiana number for a cat that was supposed to be in upstate New York. "Let me explain," the caller answered, when I jokingly quipped that I hoped I didn't have to drive all the way to Louisiana to get the cat.

Kimberly Usher Fall was the owner of Operation Save the WhoDatt Fur Babies, based in New Orleans. WhoDatt worked all over the Southeast with kill shelters and then repatriated these cats to adopters up north via a driver she referred to as their "cat lady." Chester, the cat that I had emailed about, was a one-year-old Maine coon mix, orange and quite playful. This was great, I said. And I was grateful that she'd called me. But I couldn't adopt a cat I'd never met; the cat was intended for my daughter, who was only four.

"Oh, don't you worry about that," she said, in a Southern drawl that made me miss the graceful liltings of my grandmother's Chattanooga accent. "We got a thirty-day money-back guarantee at WhoDatt."

I laughed out loud at this. "I don't think I want to teach my daughter that you can give animals back."

"I get that," comforted Kimberly. "You take your time about it. We have a real nice circle of folks up in New York who'll take him if y'all don't feel good about him. Y'all think on it, and I'll let you know if I get in something else."

Kimberly ended up getting in not one, but two something elses. And while these candidates were also Louisiana-based, they were kittens, which ticked off a box on Leo's wish list. First up was a black kitten named Mittens, but the day Kimberly sent me photos, she also wrote to tell me that there'd been a mix-up: Mittens was spoken for. This also happened with the second option, a queenly ragdoll, Bella Luna. In the meantime, I'd been charging ahead with applications without any results. In two months of searching, Kimberly was the only person who ever called me back.

Mittens and Bella Luna made the trip up north, but Chester was still sheltered and available in New Orleans. I started to feel like that cat was destined for us, meant, somehow, to be ours. I shared this instinct with Leo, who said that he wanted nothing to do with a cat he hadn't met. Meanwhile, Nina was working overtime on the "I want a sibling" front, so Leo's resolve was wearing thin. By March, his "no way, no how" protests had dwindled to "it's your responsibility if this thing doesn't work out."

But what could go wrong? Thanks to the horses (and the riding), I was stronger in mind and body, I was sleeping soundly, my daughter and I were reading together and grooming Harley at the barn and singing to pop music on our girly drives back home. I didn't have the insomnia monster weighing in on my decisions. My instincts were sound.

With our commitment to Chester put in writing, I followed the northward trajectory of the cat lady via a group text that Kimberly had put together for us "fur parents." There were about twelve of us on the thread that Kimberly kept updated with exclamation marks and mileage markers and lots of paw emojis. The morning of the cat lady's expected arrival, I got a text meant just for me: "There r actually 2 cats that look like yours: Chester has on a blue collar, the other 1 no collar."

Noted, I thought, as I continued cleaning out the carrier that I'd carry our new cat home in, lining it with a pee pad and a fluffy towel.

On the drive out to meet the cat lady and her kitty charges, I had a good feeling about the whole thing until I arrived at the address I'd been given for the pickup. It was one of those McMansions that look like they'll blow over in a moderate wind, its unnecessarily long driveway lined with cat-carrier-toting women who—and I'm including myself in this company—looked slightly unhinged, holding on as we were to the hope that we weren't making a mistake.

Right on time, the cat lady tore up the gravel driveway, catapulting out of the van with a booming, "Booyah!"

"I put on an adult diaper back in Virginia so I could get here straight!" she shouted, hitching up her pants. "I gotta pee something awful!"

With a lurch, she hauled the van door open, revealing cat carriers upon cat carriers, some of them overturned.

"I hit a speed bump coming in here, so some of y'all critters went flyin'." The woman hitched her pants again. "But they'll be okay!"

Then our courier scurried up the driveway, leaving us lonely hearts to find our furry halves.

I peered into a grotto that smelled of piss and feces. There were two crates one on top of the other right by the van door. The cat on top was orange, furry as all get-out, with huge pupils, a cutie of a kitten. The cat under him was underweight and shivering, with emerald dragon eyes, fur caked in dried urine and. . . a blue collar.

Oh my God, I thought, that's him. That's Chester. Leo's gonna kill me.

Next to me, a woman was on her knees in front of another carrier, shouting, "Baby, baby, baby!"

Inside the McMansion, it was a pandemonium of high hopes and deceptions. The "baby, baby, baby" woman had let her cat out of his carrier, and he'd promptly made a run for it, disappearing into the caverns of the house. His fur parent was now in tears, pulling at her hair, asking herself why she'd done that when she knew better, better, better. A female couple was in a praying position in front of another cage. "Do you think he is our Fluffy? Are you gonna be our Fluffy?" Yet another woman was facing off with her cage, literally, just staring inside it while the witch eyes of a black cat stared right back.

I looked down bewilderedly at the carrier with our adoptee inside it, unsure what to do now. The cat lady came up to me, confirming I was "Chester's mama," and handed me some paperwork attesting to the fact that I was, indeed, adopting a four-year-old stray with chin acne who had recently been operated on after a dog attack. I blinked at the paperwork in hand.

"Sorry?" I said, catching her attention before she headed to the woman who was tearing out her hair. "I was told that he was one?"

She frowned in the cat's direction. "With the strays, it's hard to tell."

"Right, but I was told he'd had a home before? I didn't know it was a street cat, that he'd been attacked?"

"You know about the thirty-day money-back guarantee, right?"

Somewhere in the melee, a woman had started crying. Oh, for God's sake, I thought. I might as well take this poor cat home. I caterpillared my cat carrier against the one that Chester had arrived in, eventually managing to get the urine-soaked creature into the new carrier by tilting up the bigger one. That was it, he was inside the thing I was supposed to take him home in. Another woman had started crying—tears of joy, I think. I signed the forms, thanked the cat lady for the grueling drive, and got the hell back to my car, where I secured Chester in the back seat, facing forward.

•

It took a full six weeks to pull a pet out of that cat. The medical problems Chester arrived with were so pervasive and so varied, Kimberly ended up refunding our adoption fee without me even asking. Chin acne that looked like a tick infection, alopecia, worms. But Chester's emotional problems were the real combatant: he'd clearly been abused and was terrified of footsteps, especially if they belonged to a male foot. He was severely underweight and not making improvements in that area, because he'd taken to living behind the washing machine, where I couldn't get him food. Silent to the point of muteness during the day, at night he'd yelp and howl and prowl the house, looking for his shelter friends. Kimberly, who became my cat coach and second therapist during those training days, told me that Chester had been fond of blankets in the shelter. I discovered that he stopped trembling when I came down for him in the middle of the night (the only time he left the washing machine), and wrapped him like a baby in the folds of my bathrobe.

True to his word, Leo wanted nothing to do with this mangy error. "I was against this; you have to deal with it." His stance as a conscientious objector might seem stubborn, even cruel, but I understood it: neither of us was getting any sleep because of Chester's nighttime shenanigans, and we were slipping back into a daytime world of bickering and snaps.

My evenings with a traumatized cat were far worse than any challenge I rose to in Nina's infancy. Chester howled and prowled on a two-hour cycle: we had to get a white noise machine so that Nina would stop waking up from his distress calls. As for Nina and this terrified animal that was supposed to be her companion, she would spend her time after school on her knees with a pen flashlight, peering behind the washing machine. When Chester finally graduated to a hiding spot underneath the guest bed, she would get down on her belly and try to pull him out. And that was when I witnessed Chester's potential, something that had been hard to unearth when he'd been squeezed behind our GE. Chester was a scaredy-cat with a good animal inside. For all the times that Nina got down and prodded him or tried to push him toward her with a wooden spoon, for the Legos she flicked his way because she thought he'd want to play with them, for the time she pulled his tail, he never once hissed or put his claws out or tried to scratch my child. There was an incredible soul inside that cat, I was sure of it. Whether he'd find the confidence to be alone at night, I was less sure.

Leo voted to lock Chester in the downstairs bathroom at night to muffle his nighttime yowls, but I got it in my head that such confinement might traumatize him further. Plus, as zombie-ish as they were making me during the workday, I felt like our nighttime meetings were allowing us to bond: the feel of Chester's trembles ceasing against my nightgown, snug beneath the folds of my thick robe, was almost worth the sleep deprivation. But not quite. As I approached the end of yet another sleepless week, the overtiredness was bringing back my anxiety and my depression. If I'd been wrong about my instincts with this cat, what else was I wrong about? I had steered my family astray, made my child's longing for a sibling worse, widened the gap between me and my husband, made nighttime a hellscape. My irritable bowel syndrome returned. I started dropping weight again; the mental progress I'd made was unraveling like a piece of yarn pulled out of a pattern that had taken years to make.

Leo started bringing up the thirty-day money-back guarantee, a white flag that wasn't about money—because we'd been refunded for our lemon—but rather about getting this cat, which was the wrong cat for our family, out of our house and life. Leo ramped up his efforts one afternoon while Nina was in school, begging for a sit-down meeting in my "office," which was what I called our bedroom during daylight hours.

"We can't go on like this. They said they'd have a good home for him elsewhere, right?"

I knew Leo was right: this couldn't continue. I was jagged with sleep loss, gaunt and frazzled. I couldn't think straight. After three weeks without quality sleep, I couldn't even drive.

"But what will that say to Nina?" I worried. "She'll think everything is replaceable. I can't believe we have to do this."

"She'll understand what it looks like to make a mistake."

I gulped. I nodded. I could feel in my belly that it was what we had to do. And then our bedroom door creaked open, and Chester, who had never entered our bedroom before, much less voluntarily entered any space that had my husband in it, came into the room, moseyed down the three steps to the couch where we were sitting, rubbed his head against my husband's knee, and got into his lap.

We looked at each other, gobsmacked.

"Does he speak French?" my husband asked, because we'd been conversing in my husband's native tongue.

"He is from New Orleans."

Leo tried to pet Chester—he'd never gotten close enough for Leo to do so, before. He didn't flinch, he purred.

"Okay," said Leo, flattered. "We'll give it another day, then, see if this is a phase."

When my daughter got off the bus that day, Chester came to meet her in the kitchen. While she took her backpack off, he rubbed against her legs. He cuddled on the couch with her and let her tell him a story from a picture book while she stroked his fur the wrong way. Chester changed. He blossomed. He needed patience with his fears. It's amazing what can happen if you respect a being's fears.

29

RUNNING FREE

In April of 2017, Simsbury Polo closed for a few months while Coach Alison played the spring season down in Aiken, South Carolina, again. My second novel published to great press and sluggish sales. With a Twitter feed essentially elected president, the news cycle had become a form of entertainment: if people read, they read nonfiction, rabbit holing deep into biographies and autobiographies and treatises and Twitter threads, trying to understand how we had gotten from point A to B: Obama to Donald; marriage equality back to Proposition 8; the glass ceiling repaired.

I don't deal well with disappointment. I am not somebody built with the fortitude it takes to shrug off stagnant book sales. But something beautiful was on offer to me now: I had a way out of my own head. While before I'd nursed bad news with a run or a bike ride, physical time-outs that gave me maybe thirty minutes of headspace, now I had two to three hours in which to absolutely disappear.

Horseback riding takes a lot of time and dedication, but curiously, barn time made me more productive in my writing, not less. Since my student days, I've been on the same energy cycle: I'm productive and alert between 8:30 AM and 2:00 PM, and then I'm good for nothing. What this schedule had meant for me as a self-employed writer was that I spent the last hours of each afternoon faffing about on social media, gleaning bits of information that made me feel inadequate, overlooked, jealous, or depressed, which meant I moved into post-primary-school "mom time" from a bitter place.

Barn time cut that out. Around 1:30 PM I'd end my workday, quickly putting together whatever leftovers we had in between two pieces of bread that I would stuff in my face as I drove the twenty minutes to Pie Hill. When I pulled into the driveway that ran ninety degrees across a mountain and parked my car in front of the beautiful gray barn, it was time to leave whatever perceived slights or failures that I felt inside of the Nissan we'd bought to replace our totaled car. While I could get away with a run or bike ride with "poor me" thoughts inside my head, the horses wouldn't have it. If I didn't leave my worries behind, the horses pricked their ears at my arrival, and then I'd watch it happen, the hesitant, slow pinning of those same soft ears, the consensus of a group decision: "This woman is *stressed*." I wanted a smile from my horse friends, I wanted their ears forward. And so I learned, little by little, to stop hanging on to disappointments in favor of embracing the positive things in my life, of which there were so many.

After the barn, I would whiz home to meet Nina's school bus at the corner of our road.

"Hmmm, you smell like horses, Mama," she'd say as she hugged me by our mailbox. Because I did smell like horses, I'd draw a bath for the both of us, effectively turning what used to be one of our greatest battles into quality time. Leo would prep dinner while we bathed, and Chester would poke his orange paw under the bathroom door, riddled with FOMO. Nina kept a plastic bag of Legos under the bathroom sink that she hauled into the bath, a practice I found grody but got on board with because it brought her so much pleasure.

"You be Lea, and I'll be Frankie," Nina would say, doling out the Lego character that I was meant to be that day. "Frankie is going to jump onto her horse from the cliff now," she'd say, pushing a horse figurine through the sudsy water to me so that I could make sure that Frankie—who was named for Nina's best friend—would make it safely onto the horse's waiting back.

I didn't look at my phone in the bath with my daughter, and I didn't look at it while I showed Nina how to cut scallions and carrots and properly dose soy sauce to complement the meal that Leo had started while we were washing up. I didn't look at it while we played Old Maid and Leo instructed Nina how to chest her cards, and then it was time to get Nina to sleep and I'd gone so long without gaping at the shiny wrapping paper of other people's lives that I decided to go longer without the time suck of my cell phone, eventually settling on a system where I checked social media three times a week for a half hour, and that was it, no late-night cheating, no surfing overtime. Removing my ability to scrutinize other people's perceived successes made me less interested in analyzing my own, and so—rather incredibly, for someone capable of bewailing burnt toast for several hours—I moved past the disappointment of my underperforming novel.

•

When publishing-related doubts did manage to push their way past my emotional strongholds, I had Paugussett to disappear to: it was the glittering underworld of my fairy tales of yore. I'd graduated to ponying three horses on the gallop track, and had received compliments on my improved canter. I'd learned that just a little bit of slouch—curving my body into a C shape—allowed me to move with the horse's movements naturally. The minute I stiffened or tried to adopt dressage shoulders, I'd bounce in my seat. Around and around the gallop track we'd go, the thudding of hooves a muffler to any doubts inside me. Silence, a certain kind of silence, flooded in and I paid attention to the horse's breath, to mine, to the pace that we were keeping as we went around the track.

Carlos continued to show me small attentions before riding, but I was growing uncomfortable with his ministrations. Anyone with eyes could see that Carlos tacked faster than I ever could, but was I leading him on by letting him help me with my horse? One morning, I showed up for our warm-up laps in a tank top, and he got very close to me, complimenting me on the way it looked in Spanish. I knew enough Spanish to respond with an insistence that he take it down a notch: "*¡Cálmate!*" I said. I registered two things from his reaction: that we both knew that I knew he'd like that tank top, and that our game, whatever it was, had come to an end. We would find our way back into a tense friendship, but Carlos never put a saddle on a horse for me again.

From time to time—I never knew when we'd be gifted with it—Victor would let us play a pickup polo game in the arena. We'd bring our ponied horses back to the barn and add wraps to the ones we'd saddled, tie their tails up, tighten girths. Leah, Victor, and Carlos would change from their sneakers into polo boots. Mallets in hand, with one deflated ball, we'd head into the arena, the men fighting to be on the team with us girls.

I usually rode Pajita, the dependable mare who knew when she was dealing with an amateur and wouldn't kick into high gear unless I carried a whip. The grooms didn't adjust their playing speed because there was a newbie in their midst, and I quickly learned what fouls looked like from watching Danny make all of them. Playing at a faster pace with the players making both good and bad moves allowed me to better feel and see what I'd been doing wrong at Simsbury. I was behind the action most of the time—at a lope to the grooms' gallop—and thus I could actually see the imaginary line of the ball, could comprehend the danger that came from someone crossing it, could feel endangered, myself. I watched how the grooms swiveled with their mallets, observed the way they sat in their polo saddles—they didn't, they were always out of them, ready to pivot, twist, or hook. Their heels were down, their form impeccable, even in a frantic game. I reveled in the glory of a properly executed "bump," when one rider would crash into another to push that rider off the line, and thrilled to every ride-off, the riders' kneecaps knocking, elbows digging into the waistline of the other player, too sharply to be nice.

I learned to ride dirty at Paugussett: watched as Carlos reached across his own horse to grab Danny's reins to slow his horse down, saw Victor tug the opponents' mallets this way and that with his own stick. And although a lot of that dirty work would have got a foul called in a proper match, what it nevertheless showed me was that polo, if you surrendered to it, could be full of fun and joy, and the best way to enjoy it was to let the horses run.

"Just let them *go*," Victor said to me during a practice as I fought my horse's instincts yet again. "It'll get worse if you try to stop them," added Danny, racing by me, noting the head tossing and bit pulling of the horse I was trying to slow down. In my riding efforts, I struggled perennially with death grip—regardless of the discipline, I used my hands to communicate first, before remembering my legs. This is annoying for any horse, because your hands are connected via the reins to the soft part of the palate, but it is particularly undesirable in polo where the horse's job is to keep on moving forward. Tugging on the reins gives the horse the opposite information: it tells them to slow down.

"You're confusing them," Carlos said to me, making a "stop/go" motion with his hands. I've always felt that limbo is an excruciating place to dwell—so I was deeply ashamed that I was confusing my own mount to such a degree that Carlos, who had avoided speaking with me since our tank top run-in, had to point this out. "Be direct," "Take charge," "Let them know who's boss": these were commands continually leveled at me that summer, and although I knew that they were true—a horse does calm down when he knows that you're in charge—I was an impostor, and the horses knew it. You had to be talented to take charge, didn't you? Or was it just that you had to be a man?

On the drives home from Paugussett, I'd consider the ways that I was socialized to think of horses as a child: pretty, mystical beings whose manes were there to braid, horses that, instead of gentling, I was gentle with. What did men do with toy horses? Jump them, break them, bash them around? It was easy enough for the grooms to tell me that I had to show the horses who was boss; in their male bodies, they'd been approaching other bodies and situations as a "boss" their entire lives.

In my career, I'd been able to make the mental switch from submissiveness to girlboss: I was outspoken about my professional desires; I advocated for my writing and was proud of my ambition. But convincing myself that I was physically a leader was something else entirely.

In addition to Pajita, there was another mare that I was put on, a mahogany horse named Rosa. That summer she was constantly in estrus, and the grooms found it hysterical to give me the menstruating mare to groom. The problem was that when she was in heat, she was a liability. Rosa craved close contact when she was menstruating, and would often press me against the walls of her stall with all her force, which, at sixteen hands, was significant. One time, it was actually dangerous—she pushed against me with everything she had, crushing my lungs and chest. I had to call out with the air left in me. One of Victor's nephews came, an on-again, off-again groom named Manuel.

"Why does she do that to me," I asked, catching my breath after, my released heart racing fast. "To me, and not to you?"

"She thinks you are a stallion," he said, handing me a whip.

•

That summer, I started attending the high-goal weekend matches at Paugussett without fail; Leo liked to watch the dizzying games with me, and Nina loved running after stray balls with a foot mallet when the play was stopped, but the optics of grass polo were difficult to absorb. Watching Victor's staff—my friends now—tend to players who had a mere ounce of their natural talent made me feel complicit in the class and race hierarchies that were being erected (or rather, reinforced) with steadfast materials. The then president's persecution of Latinx people was flagrant in 2017, but it would only worsen. Like most Democrats I knew, I'd been donating to resistance causes, writing letters to senators, making phone calls, and signing dozens of petitions every day, but it didn't feel like enough. It didn't feel like anything, actually: What sweat was it off my back to send emails from a desk chair? I decided to try and learn Spanish, formally. It seemed like a meaningful action that would have an impact I could track.

Finding a teacher or conversation class in my small town turned out to be harder than I'd imagined: the group classes I found were in Hartford, over an hour away. I settled on a remote teaching program called TakeLessons and selected a Texas-based Colombian instructor named Hilda Rueda who also spoke French, as I did (so I thought she'd understand some of the French-born mistakes I made), and who was an artist, which allowed me to fantasize about us having conversations about the ups and downs of the creative life, *en español.*

Our lessons were every Thursday morning via video chat, a format I felt uncomfortable with because it made my nasolabial folds loom larger than life, but from my first lesson with Hilda, I was determined to reach proficiency in Spanish. Hilda seemed to possess the same unquestioning confidence in my abilities that connected me to Victor and the others at the barn: You might not be great at this right now, but you can get better. She encouraged me to search for my words in Spanish, question her in Spanish, take as much time as I needed to get a sentence right. I told her stories about my *gato*. Hilda loved hearing about Chester's progress in our family and would clap—"*¡Que lindo!*"—when he sashayed into the background of my screen.

Learning Spanish absorbed whatever free time remained in my work and home life: I wrote, I rode, I parented, I spoused, I friended to my friends, and I *hablé española*. With no time for the overanalyzing of minutiae, my mental outlook kept improving, as did my creativity.

When the horse needs to run, you let it. Without my lesser self yanking on my own reins, I was writing with a freedom and a jubilance I hadn't experienced since I was younger. I wrote as if I were trying to summon something, bring a body back from the dead. Horseback riding had shown me how to give myself completely to a pursuit, and—in gratitude for how much the horses were helping me with my writing—I tried to bring this exuberance and blind faith back to them.

I was saddled to a horse named Macarena when I finally achieved this. Macarena was the smallest of the Paugussett polo string and by far the cutest: she had a mischievous pony attitude to her, and the largest eyes. But she was rumored to be *fast*. When Victor told me to tack her for a pickup game, I felt I'd won a prize: I must be improving if I got to ride that mare.

At the beginning of the game, I commenced my fretful tugging at the leather reins, but I listened this time when Victor told me to stop holding her back. I leaned into the action, tore into the train, stole the ball from Danny, allowed myself the fun. I felt for the first time what it was like to be in harmony with what the horse wanted to do. We were going fast, yes, and it was okay. I was mounted, I was happy. I was freed—if only temporarily during a morning in July—from the clench of my worst instincts.

In the iconic riding instructor and writer Sally Swift's *Centered Riding*, she writes about just such a moment, the triumph of the freewheeling right brain over the left brain's micromanaging:

> *Have you had times of physical activity when your body gave you pure joy, when what you did seemed infinitely easy and correct? . . . These are the breakthrough moments when the right brain is allowed to take over the responsiveness of your body with no interference from the left.*

God, I thought, this is what it probably feels like to my daughter when she's allowed to take the time she wants to dress herself and eat. This is what it feels like to my husband when I'm not dialoguing with him through a checklist: Did you do this? Did you do that? And did you do it right?

I had to let up on the reins, both the real and the metaphorical. I had to let the proverbial horses *go*. It is a known fact that horses run best when they don't have a rider.

30

TEQUILA

The summer sauntered on, succulent and quiet. Whenever doubt knocked, I'd go to the barn to visit Harley, or make plans to rise the following morning at five to make it to Paugussett. Alison had returned from Aiken, so arena polo was in session, and I was pleased to see that all my riding with the Paugussett crew had made me a better player. But speed still made me nervous, an issue that came into stark relief one morning in September.

It was an early morning like any other at the upstate club: Danny, Carlos, Victor, Leah, and I were readying the ponies for the gallop track. I was put on a horse I'd never ridden named Tequila, who, from the moment we left the stable, nerved and twitched beneath me with unbridled energy. I could feel her exuberance and restlessness through my tack as we danced out of the barn with the extra horses at our side.

"I've got a runner," I yelped, hoping that if I voiced my fear, I'd be better equipped to fight it. But true to form, none of the grooms acknowledged my doubts, because it would only coddle those doubts into becoming an actual problem. Victor had told me time and time again that he would never put me on a horse I couldn't handle, and I reminded myself of that as we headed out to the track, repeating another mantra that Alison was always yelling at me: "Believe, Courtney! Believe!"

Believe and breathe, I thought. Don't let her feel you're anxious. But Tequila's energy only mounted as we approached the racetrack. I was too embarrassed by a scenario in which we all had to turn back so that I could switch horses to try speaking up again. Inconveniencing my friends was a greater mortification than having mounted an animal that was too much horse for me.

But once we hit the track, I knew I was in trouble. Tequila's head was high, her steps prancy. Her mouth pulled at the bit and her body surged. I managed to control her at the walk, but as our trot approached our fourth lap, when we habitually moved into the canter, she strained at the tack. We burst into a canter that soon became something else in the slow-but-fast-moving way you recall an accident. I can still feel my own reckonings with the quickening pace: This is fast, but is this too fast? Yes, it is too fast. We were racing by this point, Tequila, a high-goal polo pony, at a professional-grade gallop, faster than that, actually, because she had my panicked legs goading her on. Later, the grooms would tell me that I was clenching her too tightly: when the going gets rough, *that's* when you relax. This proved to be a challenge on the gallop track with three horses on a line.

Around and around we went, the other barns' grooms yelling out, "*¡Más despacio!*" as we whizzed by. "*¡Tengo un problema!*" I knew enough to answer. "I'm in trouble!" I called out to Danny when I overtook his string, as well. My team's speed was worsening, not slackening. I had so many horses with me and we were going so fast: whatever accident befell me, it was going to be bad. I hadn't known slow, predictive fear like that since I saw the tree our car was headed for during our pivotal crash, a fear nearing hysteria, a fear so belly-deep it almost made me laugh. If I fell at the speed that we were going at, I would be trampled, if not by my own ponies, then by one of the strings behind me. I tried to breathe but couldn't. My body was ramrod-straight, my chest pitched forward (which only made those horses faster), my belly in my throat, all signals of distress that further freaked the horses. We were tearing up the gallop track, pushing by the other grooms, several of whom had come to a full stop to try and sort out what to do. Even though the nylon lead lines were cutting into my hands, I refused to drop the ropes. I couldn't lose those horses—they could run off, panicked, toward the main road, injuring themselves or someone in a screeching car. I figured if we just kept circling the track, Tequila would eventually stop, wouldn't she? But she was a trained polo mount, trained to go until she dropped—literally—to the ground; if I couldn't stop her, she might not stop herself.

We were going so fast my eyes were tearing, every pace forward a new launch down a roller coaster. My stomach felt as if it had been hollowed out and replaced by an eel that was sucking at me and electrocuting me at the same time. I looked down the far side of the arena where the entrance gate was, wondering if I couldn't figure out a safe way to fall, when I saw that Carlos had halted his horses and was arranging all six of them in a line across the track, effectively creating a wall out of horseflesh. Tequila knew these horses, exercised every day with them. She wouldn't recoil in terror, and there wasn't a path forward—I couldn't jump my string of horses over Carlos's. We would have to stop. We did.

I was choked up when we halted, from fear of course, but also from the realization that one of those grooms was going to lead me back to the barn, watch me put away the horses, and tell me that I could never ride with them again. My proud cover was blown— everyone on the track that day had seen what an amateur I was.

But that wasn't what happened. Victor had me ride the same string of horses behind him and Danny for a few laps at the canter. That was all he said: "Again. You get behind us and you do it again." This approach to riding—the get-back-in-the-saddle attitude—is something that separates horse enthusiasts from real horse people for me. It feels callous when it happens to you—my heart was racing, my pulse still in my throat as we picked up that canter—but making me do the exercise over was a public act of forgiveness and inclusivity, a nod to the fact that we all lose control and make mistakes, sometimes. That what had happened was part of riding, that it wasn't a big deal. That they let me keep riding with them, that was the big deal.

"What happened, nothing happened," Carlos said, shrugging, when I flouted our new rules and hugged him once we'd dismounted at the barn, thanking him for nothing less than the saving of my life. "*No pasó nada*," he repeated, blushing. "You stayed on."

And I did stay on. I didn't let the horses go. "You were going *fast*," Danny laughed. "I would have let go of them. It's because she had her grain." He pointed to the bucket Tequila had been eating out of before I rode her.

"It's because you were gripping her," said the less euphemistic Victor, who accompanied this statement with a grimace and fists curled. "You have to . . . relax. Breathe, you let go a little. Don't hold on to them so tight."

My rigidity and panic were a disappointment to us both. I wanted so terribly to break on through to the other side, to a place where I could become relaxed in the face of fear. I wanted to build up to a riding ability where the more unsettled my mount was, the calmer I became. Where I sat back instead of forward in tense moments, and breathed fluidly instead of holding on to breath.

Victor—ever the intuitive when it mattered—could see that I was near tears. "You need to get better, and you're not riding a donkey," he said, reaching for a post-ride beer out of a cooler. "These horses have blood. You have to be more open." He reached across the trash barrel that separated our chairs and touched two fingers to my heart. "You have to be more open *here*."

31

FIRE HORSE

In her first-grade class that fall, Nina was working on nonfiction writing and the elements of storytelling. "Gymnastics with Frankie," "My Birthday by Nina," and "My First Time at Target," were some of the tomes she brought home in her backpack, stapled papers featuring blond-haired stick figures doing cartwheels, traveling in wheeled boxes, or singing musical notes.

"I used to make books too," I told Nina, looking through her stories. "Just like this, with words and pictures. Do you want to see them?"

Nina followed me upstairs, twisting impatiently as I examined my bedroom shelves for my own set of stapled books. I knew exactly where they were, but I was stealing time. Nina was embarrassed by her writing; she got emotional when she had to write something because she didn't think that her handwriting was any good. I remembered having solid handwriting when I was in first grade, and I worried it might dishearten her, seeing that I'd illustrated and written my stories in a steadier hand than hers.

But when I finally pulled out the collection of my girlhood books, I had a shock. The little books I had been certain that I'd written as a seven-year-old had, in fact, been transcribed from whatever scribbles I'd handed in, into the teacher's more legible hand. Indifferent to my realization that I wasn't the writing prodigy I'd remembered myself as, Nina reached for the books.

"You got to put pictures anywhere you wanted?" she asked in amazement. In Nina's books, the illustration placeholder was clearly demarcated at the top of the page, with lines for her prose below. Mine had unicorns and Pegasuses drawn at the far corners of the pages and in the middle of the text.

"You can do whatever you want with stories," I told her, pulling out another book that I'd loved as a child, *A Light in the Attic* by Shel Silverstein. "He's got a drawing on every single page too," I said, reading Nina a few of the poems I'd so loved as a child, the silly verses about unfunny clowns, grouchy pirates, and polar bears in Frigidaires.

Nina's eyes went wide. This was freedom: stories, storytelling, drawing, erasing, the creation of anything you wanted on a blank page. Complete and utter freedom. Already, Nina had started to grasp that you could tell true stories through songwriting (she was on #TeamSelena after having listened to both Selena Gomez's and her ex-boyfriend Justin Bieber's breakup songs), but the fact that you could make fiction—create new worlds with artistic license—was still dawning on her.

Our car trips back and forth to Pie Hill were the site of Nina's most fervent research into the differences between fact and fiction. She wanted to understand the lyrics to Leonard Cohen's "Hallelujah" ("What does 'baffled' mean?" "Why'd she cut his

hair?"), and she had all kinds of theories as to what the performer
Sam Smith was referring to when they sang that their ex could
take off with their "diamonds." She'd chew on her half of the
cheese-and-mayonnaise sandwiches I always made for barn trips
and ask about the dating lives of stars I didn't know. Why didn't
Justin love Selena anymore? Was Justin Bieber a bad man?

Love is also a form of storytelling with conflicts and cre-
scendos, and my marriage—our marriage—was on a brand new
chapter. Leo and I had quit our couples therapy after five or
so sessions—partly, the drive became too long after our move
to Connecticut, but also, after we lost the pregnancy, we were
able to speak to each other with kindness because we had been
through something difficult as a united team. Even though we
hadn't stuck with it very long, we got what we needed from
counseling, which was the ability to call upon a referee when our
words turned dangerous. "It's the way life goes, sometimes," I
explained to my daughter, who was convinced that Selena Gomez
and Justin Bieber were better together than apart. "People can
fall out of love with each other, and then fall back in love again."

•

The Christmas holidays were approaching, and as we hadn't seen
Leo's French family in a year, we decided to stay abroad for two
months and teach Nina from home. I was excited to return to
my in-laws', stronger, kinder, and healthier than I'd been the year
before. My mother-in-law, Annie, was someone special to me, a
highly intuitive woman who marked each of our visits by leaving
a special item of her clothing or jewelry on the bed for our arrival.

"This is just an old thing of mine," she'd say, nodding at some fabulous caftan or tunic spread across the comforter, "and you probably won't like it" (she knew that I would like it), "but *voilà*, there you go."

I loved these small surprises. Annie's gifts—though sometimes eccentric—made me feel that she saw me trying to be more relaxed and sensual than I currently was; that she saw, in fact, my desire to be a caftan kind of girl.

The arena matches leading up to my departure were fun, but bittersweet—we had new members on the team whom I was growing close to and was going to miss. Alison called the members of our hodgepodge team her "polo family," and family was what it was starting to feel like. Melanie, a new member, was a retired electron microscopist with a daughter who was a rising polo star on the collegiate scene. Like me, Mel—as she preferred to be called—feared out-of-controlness, and her marriage was showing cracks. Phyllis, who had joined our team around the same time as Melanie, was an overnight pharmacist in a local hospital, a parent to a dog named Pumpkin, and the best friend of an Ohio-based twin sister she dearly missed. Much like my mother-in-law, Phyllis was quiet but intuitive, and boundlessly kind. When she found out my birthday had passed, she gifted me a beautiful hand towel created by a group she was a part of that teaches weaving to the blind. She told her book group about my writing, and traveled to my book talks even though she should have used the free time she had to catch up on her sleep. My polo team, in fact, began asking me questions about the projects I was working on and—in the case of the younger players—sussing out whether my first novel was too spicy for them to read. True to form as someone who championed the person in the player, whenever we had a new person playing with us, Alison would canter around the ring at warm-ups, pointing at us members with her polo mallet and hollering our accolades: "She's the head of the Hartford Hospital pharmacy department!" "She shows Arabian horses!" "He's in a robotics class!"

My polo team gave me something I hadn't had since I was little: unadulterated play. Even though we were playing and riding at different levels, we were all united by the same impractical desire to get good at a weird sport. My teammates made me laugh, and it was a laughter that was innocent—existing outside the point system I sometimes assigned at home (Leo noticed my new sweater, we are not getting divorced; I can't get my daughter to smile at me, two points off for this disaster). Because it really was funny, four generations of players from wildly different backgrounds trying to play *polo*. A lot of things went wrong. Jared had one speed in his arsenal—the gallop—and a tendency to forget to tighten his girth before he mounted, which resulted in his tack bursting apart once while he was crashing through the train. Nelson was a college student from China who used his mallet like an airplane propeller, a whirring hazard to all, but he had burgeoning life lessons that were a riot to listen to ("If you want to get good grades in college, you have to eat space food because it has all the essential nutrients you need and takes three minutes to eat and digest, saving you an hour for each meal that you don't spend in the mess hall"). Lizzie continued to ride circles around all of us, criticizing me for my laborious turns ("You're doing, like, these wide dressage turns. You've got to *spin*") and reminding me, as Alison did, to play defense once in a while.

I was also going to miss what we had dubbed our "team meetings" after practice, when those of us old enough to would gather at a local restaurant to recap that night's game, gossiping about bad hooks and hot horses and which of us Nelson had almost decapitated with his lawless mallet.

The only teammate of mine on social media was Lizzie, so while I was in France, I broke my three-times-a-week social media rule to hover over her Instagram posts and see what I was missing back home. Popcorn had been "bucky" on Monday but Lizzie had worked her out of it; Clark had had some issues with a rearing mare named Samba; Alison had forced Nelson to play without a mallet for a chukker because he was still doing high hooks. I checked Lizzie's feed on Mondays and on Wednesdays, the two nights she played. On a Thursday evening, I realized I hadn't looked at her post the night before, so I opened my Instagram application while Nina and Leo were downstairs, helping Annie prepare a meal of white wine mussels and french fries that we'd been looking forward to.

"RIP Popcorn," Lizzie's static post read, followed by a fleet of black hearts and crying emojis.

I blinked at the image of the picture-perfect horse, searching for an explanation, but no one else had commented. I opened up direct messages and wrote her right away. Popcorn was Lizzie's favorite horse, the one she nearly always rode. Compact, fast, and furious, Popcorn could turn on a half dime and went from zero to forty in seconds. I'd ridden Popcorn twice and had been looking forward to riding that spirited horse again when I got back.

"What happened??" I wrote Lizzie. "Popcorn DIED?"

The dot dots made my heart quicken—she was typing her response. "They all died," the message came. "Didn't you hear?"

And then Lizzie disappeared—I was six hours ahead and it was a school day for her, but I nevertheless stared into my phone desperate to see the dot dots reappear. Leo yelled up the stairs to ask what I was doing—it was french fry–cutting time.

"One second!" I yelled back.

I grabbed my computer and Googled "Simsbury Polo Club." The response loaded slowly; the connection wasn't good. But then the answer was there in front of me, one result after another saying the same thing. The previous night in a freak electrical accident, the Simsbury Polo Club had burned to the ground.

Over the next few days, through phone calls and WhatsApp messages to the players and news clips cropping up, I pieced together what had happened. Sometime between the evening check-in at 11:30 and the morning check at dawn, an arc from a grounded outlet had shorted in the utility room adjacent to the riding school's tack room. The hot wire didn't trigger the barn's heat sensor system because there weren't any flames, but it did create a lethal amount of smoke. That night in Simsbury, it was minus five degrees Fahrenheit. The doors and stall windows that would have been cracked open on a milder night were sealed closed. A small mercy: none of the horses burned because the flames weren't catalyzed until the early morning when a groom opened a side door and unknowingly let oxygen into the closed barn. By that time, it was too late to save the animals: the horses had died of asphyxiation overnight. Twenty-four horses in all—including our entire polo school string. When the fire department screeched up to the building, the water lines were frozen. They saved what they could of the arena and the barn.

Some of my teammates lived close enough to have seen Alison—they said not to contact her on the phone yet, she was too distraught to talk. She wasn't giving interviews to the newscasters crowding round the barn. Those horses had been her friends, her colleagues. She owned twenty-one of the twenty-four lost. In the year that I'd known Alison, there wasn't anything that she wasn't able to do to make a horse feel better. A veterinary surgeon by trade, she injected and wrapped and soothed and clipped and shored and stitched whatever necessary. But she hadn't been able to do anything for those frightened animals, many of which she had trained herself to be the kind of ponies that anyone could ride.

The fire horse is another Chinese zodiac sign: people born under this sign are forceful and eventful, full of passion and drama and a lust for life. As for the horses born under this sign? I sat down on the bed in my mother-in-law's fishing cottage in the northwest of France, a house that I'd been visiting—and loving—since meeting Leo so many years before, and I thought of these beings that I would never smell again, or touch. Estrella, who was the first polo pony I'd ever cantered on, so forgiving of my amateur travails, tiny, fearsome, as smart as all get-out. Samba, who wore her name well with her side-stepping and dancing. The noble and patient Kat, a killer on the straightaway, but so damn hard to turn. Popcorn, whom I'd been hoping I was good enough to ride.

In May 1910, facing a parish bewildered by King Edward VII's passing, a priest named Henry Scott Holland delivered a sermon in Saint Paul's Cathedral in London called "Death, the King of Terrors," in which he asked what death was, other than a "negligible accident."

Death is nothing at all. . . . Nothing has happened. Everything remains exactly as it was. I am I, and you are you, and the old life that we lived so fondly together is untouched, unchanged. Whatever we were to each other, that we are still. . . . Laugh as we always laughed at the little jokes that we enjoyed together. Play, smile, think of me, pray for me. Let my name be ever the household word that it always was. Let it be spoken without an effort, without the ghost of a shadow upon it. Life means all that it ever meant. . . . There is absolute and unbroken continuity. . . . Why should I be out of mind because I am out of sight?

This loss, the tragedy of the arena fire, which was a tragedy for many, a loss of resources and infrastructure and investments and horses, was something that I feared would bring me back into the dark times of my saddest hours. Polo had been an outlet, an escape route from the pressures of my life at home. But although I wept as I worked my way through what the news of the fire meant, I also slept. Although I mourned, my mind did not go skittering into the tundra of anxiety. Something I had loved was gone. Beloved animals were dead. But do you know what I realized? My nights in that arena had scared me. I got hurt and I fell off and I had had so many times when I asked myself why in the hell I was making myself do something that I was afraid of, but it was because there was a cleansing in that fear. My team—the horses, the teammates, Alison—did not let me give up on doing something I was afraid of, and I was stronger for it. The horses were gone. The arena was gone. The people were not gone.

When Alison surfaced, she pledged to rebuild. Polo clubs and organizations up and down the coast drummed up horses to lend her, and donations poured in from people who had never even been to Folly Farm. On the club's social media pages, people who understood the healing power of animals—not just horses—mourned the loss of beings who were innocent, and noble, and, quite simply, good.

The drowning horse in my favorite childhood film, *The NeverEnding Story*, was a horse that died in my child's mind, died never to come back, died in a way that was terrifying and broke the rules of storytelling (the hero's animal companion isn't supposed to *die*). My adult self understands now that that horse didn't die. In actuality, there were two Artaxes, two white horses trained to be Atreyu's faithful mount. Both horses were put on an elevated lift week after week and trained not to panic as they were submerged in mud. You can watch the scene online: the horse's ears aren't fully pinned back until the child actor is screaming at him, the horse's body nearly completely drowned in mud. This is such an incredible feat, not just on the horse trainers' part but on the part of the horses themselves. To go again and again into a terrifying situation trusting that the worst thing won't come to pass. That level of abandonment and blind faith in another. That's real trust. That's love.

While looking for a way to mentally process what had happened at Simsbury, I came upon a saying online that is attributed to both the Indian author Sri Ram and the American "6-Figure Speaker" Brian Tracy. Despite the quotation's shady provenance, it nevertheless brought me solace: "You cannot control what happens to you, but you can control your attitude toward what happens to you, and in that, you will be mastering change rather than allowing it to master you."

After the Simsbury fire, life meant all that it ever meant, it had all the potential that it had ever had, it still had beauty in it. There were still horses out there to scratch and carrot-feed and nuzzle, to brush and ride and care for, to love and lose and mourn. Even out of sight, I could hear the horses run.

32

I BELIEVE IN MAGIC

"I was right! Behold the MERMAID!" On the TV screen, the actor Eugene Levy is spraying a supine Daryl Hannah with a water hose. Flashbulbs clack and the crowd erupts in screams. Hannah's human legs are puckering and scaling, conjoining to fin. The truth is out there. This beautiful blond woman, such a hit at the party they are there for, is actually a fish.

I'm holding my daughter's hand as we take in the pivotal scene in another one of my favorite childhood movies, *Splash*. I always get emotional when I'm sharing something with Nina that mattered in my childhood, but watching this modern mermaid tale is a powerful trip backward. Like so many things—scrunchies, Micro Machines earrings, boys with skater hair—*Splash* was something I was obsessed with until I moved on to something else. But watching this movie with my daughter reminds me of how much it meant to me as a child, the proof that everything in my imagination had the potential to be real.

I believed in unicorns when I was little, and in mermaids too. It was after watching *Splash* for the first time that I hauled a giant Hefty bag out to the pool, taped it around my waist with duct tape foraged from the garage, and hurled my unsupervised seven-year-old body in the deep end because I was convinced that the garbage bag would function as a mermaid tail once I hit the water. Instead, the Hefty bag filled with liquid, and I almost drowned. It was only from having practiced my "mermaid swim" all summer that I was able to kick my way over to the pool's edge with my legs in fin mode and pull myself hand over hand to the shallow side. I did not tell my mother what had happened, because I didn't want anybody to know that my legs had not metamorphosed into a mermaid's tail as I'd imagined, that I didn't have the mermaid magic that I thought I had.

Another time, I jumped off a staircase in that house with an umbrella because I thought that I would fly like Mary Poppins. I sprained an ankle instead. Whenever I sneaked into my father's sports car alone, as I was wont to do because it smelled of him, I would talk to the dashboard, certain that it would answer like the talking car in *Knight Rider*. And while my mermaid tail never sprouted and my dad's car didn't talk back, the magic and escapism that horses promised me in childhood kept their promise in adulthood. Adults ruin a lot of things that are beautiful and mysterious: they tell children that Santa doesn't exist, they spray water onto the legs of a woman who is trying to hide a secret so that she can be with the man she loves for six days in Manhattan, but no adults stepped in, ever, to ruin horses for me. I don't care where you stand on horses, if you set out to debunk the hold they have on people, take away their power, prove that they aren't as enchanting as they seem to be, you will lose, because they are that powerful, they are that moving, they have something that there aren't words to explain.

The year 2017 turned into 2018. The dynamics of my riding shifted and the horses aged. One day, Nina and I went to feed an aged white horse we were fond of at Pie Hill only to find that he'd been put down overnight. The chilly dampness of an early spring made Harley's arthritis worsen: he had started to stumble when I rode him, which caused me to tear up on our way home, emotions my daughter couldn't see from her booster seat behind me. He was aging, she was aging, I was aging too.

Without the Monday polo nights and team meetings that had fueled each of my workweeks, the days felt long and leaning, like books without bookends. I started making frequent walking trips to our town library to give my energy direction, and in short time, the welcoming librarians became quasi relatives. "Miss Eileen," as the children's librarian was known, took to driving bags of hand-picked books over to our house for Nina to go through when the weather was especially bad. I privately rejoiced that Miss Eileen's selections always had a feminist bent to them: a biography of the American contralto Marian Anderson; *Beatrix Potter: Scientist; Mary Wears What She Wants*, about the nineteenth-century doctor Mary Edwards Walker, who was repeatedly arrested for wearing pants. In one of these books, an illustrated story about the French American artist Louise Bourgeois, I learned the French noun *"rentrayage,"* a word that means "to reweave across the cut," or, in simpler terms, "to mend." I had recently taken a class on mending in order to salvage a moth-eaten rug I loved, and though I was familiar with the way you had to widen a garment's hole to fix it properly, bringing in extra cloth to sew onto the frayed material instead of trying to sew the ripped bits together, I hadn't heard this term.

I stole away with the book that night, taken by the idea that Louise Bourgeois had learned how to create massive, heavy sculptures by first working on the reparation of small and fragile things. Small things, small adjustments—they really made a difference. Checking to make sure that the girth running under a horse's belly wasn't pinching his skin, taking Nina's snow boot off and witnessing, as I shook it out for her, that she hadn't been exaggerating—there had been a piece of branch inside.

Mending, we were mending, all three of us, plus cat. Learning to be direct and assertive with horses had helped me to be clearer and braver regarding what I needed in my marriage. After dropping passive-aggressive hints for many years, I sat down and explained to Leo that while I understood his need to focus exclusively on the "art" part of his filmmaking, which meant taking on little to no freelance work when he was crafting something new, the pressure of being the only wage earner during those lengthy stretches was too much for me. For years, Leo had had one regular client who always drummed up freelance editing work if Leo asked, but the company had been purchased by an investment firm that replaced its freelance contractors with an advertising agency, closing that financial avenue. Could he find another way to bring in a little money, even if the gig was outside film? At least until he found a committed investor for his second feature?

Leo listened. And he acted. He got his contractor license and worked long days in the cold and drizzle, lugging broad beams into additions on vacation homes. He even picked up part-time work installing tombstones with a stone-carving friend. In the silence of the home I was working in by myself now, I was better able to recognize all of the things Leo had been doing—quietly and often unthanked—to keep our house warm in the winter and dry in the wet months. Venturing into the basement's dankness to make sure the sump pumps were holding up, and doing whatever it is one does to fix a sump pump when they weren't. Sketching, planning, and building bunk beds for our daughter to make up for the fact that, no, Nina, Mama still hadn't changed her mind about providing a sibling, but there would be plenty of sleepovers and adventures with her friends. I wanted—we both wanted—Nina to have friends so close they were like her family. It was what we both had when we were growing up. Leo's best man at our wedding was the neighboring child from the first apartment that he lived in as a toddler, and this man, Martin, remains his best friend, still.

We didn't know this yet, but soon Leo would get a phone call from the owners of an entertainment studio that would fund his entire film. We didn't know that the coronavirus was coming, nor that it would shut down years of live performances for rap artists like Freddie Gibbs, a megastar Leo had long wanted for the lead role in his movie, and was suddenly able to get. I would solo-parent for three months while Leo filmed and edited abroad, forging new traditions with my daughter such as eating buttered rigatoni together on the couch in front of *Clueless*, letting her style my hair with no less than ten barrettes, and losing to Nina, repeatedly, at Kings in the Corner card games by the fire that I dragged wood to, and cleaned of embers, and kept running by myself. We didn't know any of this, but we were better prepared to welcome these changes than we'd been a year earlier because Leo and I were weaving our way back to one another, thread by tattered thread.

On the polo front, Alison did rebuild the Simsbury Polo Club, and she brought in some wonderful new horses, including a mare named Gilda I've bonded with who is blind in one eye, dislikes standing still, and treasures candy canes. I continued to get better on arena nights. I started to go fast. I even netted myself a Most Improved Award that I couldn't accept because I hadn't known you had to be a registered member of the USPA to take home such a thing. In the meantime, I'd kept up with the Spanish, advancing to a level where I could defend myself and my abilities on the polo field. That spring, I traveled to a part of western Mexico called Careyes to research a new book, a remote but storied location where there happened to be a polo club at the foot of the house where I was staying. After learning that the American club manager didn't want me to join in a practice match because she preferred to court the wealthy homeowners who could play the entire season, I pleaded my case to the Mexican polo coach in Spanish. "I'm not as fast as the other people," I said, "but I know what I'm doing, and I'm safe." My name was on the board the next day for my first match on the grass.

There's another addition to our arena team, a polo player by passion and a roto driller by trade named Matt. On balmy Mondays after practice, some of us have beers down by the river that snakes at the club's edge, bundled up against the unpleasantness of our sweaty T-shirts, passing one of the bottle openers—a steel-plated reproduction of the Angkor Wat complex that Nelson gifted to each member of our arena team for Christmas—back and forth between us. We talk about how we did at practice, and we talk about our goals. Phyllis has just purchased three of her own ponies so that she can play at a higher level without having

to rent horses, and has picked up extra overnight shifts at the local hospital to cover her horses' board. Matt wants to make it to a
1 handicap by the year's end, a goal that will be difficult, because
he also overlooked the crucial step of USPA registration, the body
that distributes handicaps. *What about you?* they ask me at these
team meetings in the grass. *What do you want from the game?*

This question has been asked of me before. In the Careyes,
which I continued to visit as I wrote my book about surrealists,
I developed a peculiar but strong friendship with a gentleman
farmer there who goes by the name "Jimmy" because his real name
reminds him of his Germanness and the blood that connects him
to hatred and to war. When I am in Mexico, Jimmy lets me ride a
horse of his named Boogie-Woogie, stick-and-ball alongside him
on his ranch. He has no tolerance for my cautious playing; he yells
at me to *ride*. His exhortations are so convincing that I let my walls
down, and I play with confidence. I play just for play.

"What is your goal?" he asked me while we were drinking
Coronitas under a *palapa* on his property after playing one-on-
one. "What do you want to do?"

Jimmy said that I had talent. If I had a horse or two of my
own, regular training, I could be good.

"I just want to play like this," I said, nodding toward the tidy
arena bordered by Montezuma cypress trees, the hosed-off horses
munching grass. "Play like this, sometimes."

This infuriated Jimmy. After all, he had organized the latter part of
his life—he was seventy-two when we were having this conversation—
around the acquisition, maintenance, and training of his polo string
and the development of his horsemanship. To play just for play's sake,
without a goal in mind, was anathema to him.

"Listen," I said, calling up the defense I'd used in similar conversations. "It's also a money thing. There aren't any grants for female polo players my age—it's not like the high school and college levels. I'll never be good enough to have somebody pay me to play, ever. Buying a horse isn't the problem." Jimmy knew as well as I did that once you were in the horse world, the promise of a cheap horse—or even a free horse—was never far away. The one-time purchase of a horse wasn't the financial obstacle; it was the upkeep. The farrier and veterinarian bills. The sky-high East Coast board.

Jimmy opened another beer, digesting my answer. He saw the logic in what I was saying, but logic didn't make up the whole truth.

"You have to understand," I said, twisting at my bottle cap. "It's a point of pride for me, also. That this is enough. I just want to have fun out there. Polo makes me happy. This is all I want."

Jimmy looked at me askance, but I knew he understood. This was a man who had been painting all his life, painting big and painting beautifully, but who detested with every fiber of his being when he was pressured by someone in the art world to "sell" or "show." He didn't respect my lack of ambition in the polo arena, but he certainly respected that I needed one area of my life to be a safe place, free from the pressures and the market forces that beleaguered, sometimes—and fueled at others—my creative life.

A safe place that just so happened to be one of the most dangerous sports in the world.

33

BIBLIOGRAPHY

My adult body is wedged between two portable fans, my husband's sack of digital camera equipment, and four boxes of manuscripts in the closet of our guest room, where we keep the life refuse that doesn't fit anywhere else.

I'm looking for the term paper I wrote about my brother's medical condition my junior year of high school. The boxes I'm going through are large and black, filled with story drafts and research papers and press clips alongside ziplocked bundles of letters from the feverish best friendships and romances I've scorched throughout the years.

I find what I am looking for in the final box: "The Medical History of Brendan Tyler Maum, May 26, 1996, for Mr. Van Atta, AP US History."

I remember Mr. Van Atta—how could I forget him? He was a peculiar, wiry man with an old-timey mustache and a fondness for western bow ties in the Colonel Sanders vein. That May had been a crucial month in an important year: for most of us high school students, junior spring was our last chance to dazzle college admission boards with whatever cards we were still holding. With summer break around the corner, a single school day—a single hour—pulsed with the reminder that we were in make-or-break times.

Mr. Van Atta's history class was a microcosm of the possibility, excitement, and stress that we juniors were going through. It was a mixed classroom—in high school, Greenwich Academy and Brunswick merged certain courses to provide students with a coed experience before we entered the real world, where men and women were very mixed indeed.

Mr. Van Atta's grade sheet is slipped inside the plastic cover of my bygone research paper. He commended me on my "personal detachment in telling the story." I received an A. Later, much, much later, I would return to Greenwich to read from my debut novel at the local library, and Mr. Van Atta would be in attendance, along with my English teacher too.

I had stuck a photograph onto the cover of the report just under the header, and upon seeing it glued there, I remember the moment vividly. It's a scene from Christmas, this one in the Shore Road house my mother moved to after the divorce. My brother, who was around eight at the time, is all bones and length, his green flannel pajamas hitched up to reveal his slender wrists. He has a limp mullet in the photo—not my work, as I was years past forcing my amateur haircutting skills on him. Brendan is smiling in the photo, and the thing is, looking at the photo now, I think he looks happy. He has a dreamy look on his face—he's staring not at the wrapped present on his lap but at the forest of presents underneath the tree in front of him. Our mother, regardless of what was happening in her life or in ours, always made sure that there was a veritable smorgasbord of presents under the tree each year: one side of the tree for Brendan, the other side for me.

When I stuck this photo on my research paper as a seventeen-year-old, I didn't think my brother looked happy: I thought he looked thin, sick, helpless, alone. I was going for the effect of that, I'm sure of it: *Look at my poor brother.* But he wasn't alone, he wasn't. My mother would have taken nineteen bullets for him and my new stepmother was a bulldog, the first to raise hell when Brendan was bullied for the hunched way he walked or the fact that he wasn't allowed to play contact sports because a wayward ball could set off his defibrillator and cause a cardiac arrest.

I was the alone one in that photograph, and even that observation is romanticized. Perhaps it was some literary concept of solitude, but I did spend my young adult years convinced that I had to be alone to hone my talent, and that I was a lonely person: unseen, misunderstood. The problem is, the more you say that you want to be left alone by people, the more likely they are to let you. And then you are alone.

Another surprising thing about this photo: behind my brother, lugged up against the window overlooking a snow-covered backyard, is the massive wooden rocking horse that had been my fifth Christmas present, all those years ago. I had no recollection of it being there, absolutely none. It was so heavy, so cumbersome, and my mother moved so regularly, where is that thing now?

"I sold it to Mrs. Barrett," my mom said when I asked her. "When we left Old Greenwich." Mrs. Barrett was the mother of a classmate of mine whose older brother had been in the Olympics one year as a swimmer. I wondered if the former Olympian pushed his own children on it now.

That night, thinking on the fate of the wooden rocking horse, I remembered something else. My mother had made me sit for a portrait on it shortly after receiving it because she'd decided that an oil painting of me sitting on that horse would make a wonderful Christmas present for my father the following year. It was not a good experience for me. I had to sit in the cold hall in a frilly white dress, sidesaddle, with one hand holding my beloved teddy bear and the other flung somewhat carelessly over the horse's mane. I remember finding the painting creepy when it was finished. Apparently, my father didn't like it either. "He said it didn't look like you," my mom reported, when I asked if she remembered his reaction when she gave the painting to him. So why does he still have it? It's in the formal dining room of the Chattanooga home he relocated to from Greenwich, a fussy space he eats in approximately two holidays a year.

"Your mom had it done you loved the horse," my father replied in a text message. This was in response to me asking if he remembered how that painting came about, and if he had been happy with it.

"I liked it and wanted it but your mom would not let me have it."

My father is not a person who enjoys looking back. I reminded him that the painting in question was hanging in his dining room. He acquiesced: "Forgot she got horse I got painting." My mother admitted to me later that she had wanted the painting and wasn't sure how my father ended up with it. "You think I wanted the horse?" she cried. "You know how much that thing weighed?"

I texted my half brother Blake, who was still living at home in Chattanooga, to take a photo of the me-on-a-horse painting—I

wanted to look at the representation of the child that either had
or hadn't been me.

"I never realized that was supposed to be you," he promptly
replied.

A real family of communicators! "Who the hell did you think
it was?" I asked.

Blake said that because the painting hung near an old oil
painting of two brothers who were definitely not him and his
older brother, Ryan, he just assumed that the other painting was
similar, that is to say, a painting of a stranger.

I became somewhat obsessed with this painted portrait.
When I look at it now, it's not as ghastly as I remember: the artist didn't get my eyes right, or my nose, which is a pointy one
that's softened in the painting. My face is narrow when, at five,
it was plump and rounded, but the artist had an innate sense of
light and a nice way with her brushstrokes: the white dress I am
wearing gleams against the dark backdrop in a haunted way. And
although she didn't capture the meek allegiance of my beloved
teddy, the look of consternation on his wool face matches the way
I remember feeling at the time: that I might slip off the saddle in
my silken dress, sneeze, lose all blood circulation in my body, or
drop my stuffed bear to the floor. I sent the photo of the painting
to my literary agent, who is like a member of my family at this
point and appreciates weird relics from my childhood. "It looks
just like you," she said. "Your daughter's going to want this!"

Will my daughter want this stuffy, gold-framed painting that
looks either nothing like me or exactly like me, depending on
whom you ask? It is, I suppose, the ultimate portrait of my childhood; the only thing that could possibly surpass its sentimental

value is the rocking horse itself. But there's no room for the horse in our house, and my arms aren't strong enough to rock it. Plus, it isn't mine now. It belongs to someone else.

And though I suspect that the painting is too grim for Nina (she likes bright things that sparkle), she has grown to love horses, my funny, caring daughter. "She's working on a book about horse riding," Nina's second-grade teacher told me and Leo in a parent-teacher conference that, like most of everything in the year that I am writing this, took place over Zoom. "Horses seem to mean a tremendous deal to Nina. It's obviously something that she is very passionate about."

Mrs. Tallon, her teacher, promises to send one of Nina's horse stories home with her, along with her report card, on the following Monday. And while I strive to be an easygoing mom who lets her kid's inclinations develop as they come, without pushing anything on her in the form of extracurriculars, my attempts at coolness fail each time Nina brings home the kraft envelope with her report card taped inside. Her report cards have DNA in them: Is she me? Is she her father? Will she be good at something? Is she happy? Will she stay a happy girl?

Nina's report card this year says that people love working with my daughter. That she is a willing learning partner, inquisitive and keen. That she is doing excellently in gym, and math, and music, and is reading at the highest level of her grade. Okay, I think, so she's a little bit me and a lot of her own person—growing up, I loathed gym almost as much as math. The assertion that Nina is patient, social, a "collaborative" playmate, that comes from her dad.

I turn to the file in the folder that contains the horse story that her teacher promised. "Horseback Riding by Nina," reads the cover title, which someone—her teacher, presumably—typed for her in bold. Nina has painted a beautiful sky with colored markers on the cover—it looks like a sunset. At the bottom of the picture, my daughter is standing with huge hands and a red smile next to Harley, who has four straight legs, a spider body, a kind face, and a long tail. The first page of the story begins with an illustrated picture of me, my daughter, and her best friend, Frankie, whom I sometimes take along with us to the barn. "It was a sunny but cold day!" the story starts. I remember her teacher mentioning this, that Nina was focused on creating a setting, on injecting atmosphere into her writing. "Me my friend and my mom whent to the barn. My friends name is Frankie. I love Frankie. Me and Frankie were vary exited to go to the barn."

The story goes on to tell how Frankie fell in love with a former racehorse named DD—the horse I rode my first time at Pie Hill. It's true that DD used to be a racehorse, before he was a polo pony. Now he is Harley's best friend and a lover of the children who come with their horse-crazy mothers to the barn on weekends, the first one to nuzzle through your pockets to search for hidden treats, to blow hot air out of his nose appreciatively onto the heads of little girls.

I'm enchanted with the stapled piece of writing I'm holding in my hands: touched that Nina has chosen horses as a subject to spend time on, that horses and horsemanship are something that she values. But mostly, I love that Nina has drawn herself just as straight-legged and as tall as Harley, that he doesn't feel big and scary to her, that he is her peer. I love that I had managed to be open enough with my family about my need for animals that my daughter knows I love horses, and has started to love them too.

Through these majestic creatures, I had found my way back to the joyful, weird, magical, sad marrow that ran through me as a child, and I'd also found a way to reconnect with the daughter I'd lost track of. I held on to Nina's story and my eyes pricked at the hand-drawn cover. This horse, the one that brought me so much happiness, would be glorified in brown Crayola marker for all time.

"It was fun. Me and Frankie whent on the hors at the same time. Then we whent home."

The story ends like that.

ENDNOTES AND REFERENCES

PAGE 11: "New Thoughts on England's White Horse Geoglyph." Archaeology. April 24, 2017. https://www.archaeology.org/news/5506-170424-uffington-white-horse.

PAGE 23: Ende, Michael. *The Neverending Story*, trans. Ralph Manheim (New York: Puffin Books, 1993), 60.

PAGE 59: Forrest, Susanna. *The Age of the Horse: An Equine Journey through Human History*, (London: Atlantic Books, 2016).

PAGE 60: Sacred Way Sanctuary. *Native American Horse Preservation Program*. September 14, 2017. https://www.sacredway-sanctuary.org.

PAGE 61: Potter, Leslie. "Who said that? Probably not Winston Churchill." *Horse Illustrated*. January 28, 2013. https://www.horseillustrated.com/the-near-side-blog-2013-0128-winston-churchill-horse-quotes.

PAGE 64: Armijo, Ashley. "A Bit of Science Regarding Our Love of Horses." New Mexico Center for Therapeutic Riding blog post. May 12, 2016. https://www.nmctr.org/a-bit-of-science-regarding-our-love-of-horses.

PAGE 73: Ashliman, D.L. (editor). "Animal Brides and Animal Bridegrooms: Tales Told by North American Indians." https://sites.pitt.edu/~dash/animalindian.html.

PAGE 81: Knoebber, Kristen K. and Blick, Marion. Psychological evaluation (New Haven, CT: Yale Child Study Center, 1994).

PAGE 81: "What Is the Average IQ?," Healthline, last medically reviewed April 10, 2018. https://www.healthline.com/health/average-iq#average-iq.

PAGE 82: Cognitive evaluation of Brendan Maum (Greenwich, CT: Eagle Hill School, 1994).

PAGE 86: MacDonald, Dick. "The Consultants Polled by Dr. Kleinman." memorandum (New Haven, CT. Yale University School of Medicine, Section of Cardiovascular Medicine, 1995).

PAGE 121: Scott, Andrea. "Veterans with PTSD Are Turning to Horses for Healing," *Military Times*, March 7, 2018. https://www.militarytimes.com/veterans/2018/03/07/veterans-with-ptsd-are-turning-to-horses-for-healing.

PAGE 121: Thaisen, Joshua. "Horses That Heal: How Equine Therapy Is Helping People Find Peace of Mind," *Guardian*, June 23, 2015. https://www.theguardian.com/science/2015/jun/23/equine-therapy-horses-medical-treatment.

PAGE 121: "Healing with Horses," FEEL Alumni, December 21, 2015. YouTube video, 8:25. https://youtu.be/74tzgoum_pk.

PAGE 139: Linton, Eliza Lynn. "The Wild Women as Social Insurgents." *The Nineteenth Century*, 1891.

PAGE 140: Crozier, Gladys Beattie. "Ladies as Polo Players." *The Lady's Realm*, 1906. Article reprinted in *Polo Players' Edition*, May 2019.

PAGE 140: "Women in the Army: Historical Highlights, 1976." https://www.army.mil/women/history.

PAGE 140: Meagher, Colleen McInerney. *Comin' Thru: The Golden Age of Women's Polo 1934–1941.* (Mt. Pub Company Inc., 2016).

PAGE 141: Rizzo, Peter. "Marion Hollins: An Accomplished Sportswoman Was National Champion," *Polo Players' Edition*, May 2020.

PAGE 141: Hale, Stormie. *Polo's Grande Dame: The Life & Times of American Polo Pioneer Sue Sally Hale.* (Independently published, 2019).

PAGE 141: U.S. Polo Association. Cision PR Newswire. March 8, 2021. https://www.prnewswire.com/news-releases/us-polo-assn-commemorates-international-womens-day-with-the-annual-us-open-womens-polo-championship-benefitting-susan-g-komen-301241328.html.

PAGE 143: Pussywalking is a body technique developed by Sasha Cagen. You can learn more about it at https://www.sashacagen.com/pussywalking/. Billie Best is the author of the memoir *How I Made a Huge Mess of My Life (or Couples Therapy with a Dead Man)*, which regales readers with the adventures of the chickens and the Weimaraner and the cheating spouse.

PAGE 146: Johnston, Lyla June. "Yes world, there were horses in Native culture before the settlers came." *Indian Country Times.* July 3, 2019. https://indiancountrytoday.com/news/yes-world-there-were-horses-in-native-culture-before-the-settlers-came.

PAGE 156: O'Brien, Soledad. Writer and director, *The War Comes Home: Soledad O'Brien Reports* (New York: Starfish Media Group, 2014). Excerpt accessed at "The War Comes Home: Equine Therapy," Brainline: All about Brain Injury and PTSD, November 1, 2016. https://www.brainline.org/video/war-comes-home-equine-therapy.

PAGE 159: Definition of the word "folly." Britannica. https://www.britannica.com/art/folly.

PAGE 177: Aubier, Catherine. *Chinese Zodiac Signs: Year of the Horse.* trans. Eileen Finletter and Ian Murray, (London: Arrow Books Limited, 1982).

PAGE 186: Nunez, Sigrid. *What Are You Going Through.* (New York: Riverhead Books, 2020).

PAGE 190: Chapman, Gary. *The 5 Love Languages: The Secret to Love That Lasts.* (Chicago: Northfield Publishing, 2015).

PAGE 220: Swift, Sally. *Centered Riding.* (New York: St. Martin's Press, 1985).

PAGE 235: Holland, Henry Scott. "Death Is Nothing at All." (Sermon at St Paul's Cathedral, London, May 15, 1910). https://en.wikisource.org/wiki/The_King_of_Terrors.

PAGE 239: *Splash,* dir. Ron Howard, written by Babaloo Mandel, Bruce Jay Friedman, and Lowell Ganz, (Burbank, CA: Touchstone Pictures, 1984).

PAGE 241: Novesky, Amy. *Cloth Lullaby: The Woven Life of Louise Bourgeois.* (New York: Harry N. Abrams, 2016).

ACKNOWLEDGEMENTS

Thank you to my horse family: Alison, Phyllis, Melanie, Lizzie, Matt, Martín, Izzy, Ryan, Amy, Nelson, Dana. Katja. Melanie and Jimmy. Marcy, my Pie Hill Girls, and Louis. Leah, Victor, Carlos, Danny, and Manuel—I hope you know who you are and how much you helped me. Viktoria and Jeff. Ola Polo Company, Annie, Rose, Veronica. Halimah, Liz, and Kenzie.

And thank you to the horses: Harley, Gilda, Boogie-Woogie, Poker, Viggo, Flash, Despé, Cepalin, Anita, Abuelita. And Chester—honorary horse! Thank you.

My ride or die writing team: At Fletcher & Co.: Kelly, Veronica, Melissa, Christy. At WME: Sylvie. My Tin House family: Craig, Nanci, Diane, Jakob, Elizabeth, Alyssa, Allison, and Anne— thank you for heading back into the ring with me a second time. Becky, Alex, Sangi, and Gage, down the stretch we go! Norton, thank you for distributing.

Thank you to Mary Helen Bowers, Jayen Wells, @eyeout4selen3r, *Family Secrets*, and *Maintenance Phase*, whose respective online workout videos, TikTok accounts, and podcasts gave me something to hold on to (and/or laugh about) during the pandemic.

Thank you for listening, Joseph Albertario. Hilda Rueda, thank you for helping me to speak. Kimberly Usher, thank you for the cat. Chris Keyes and Eileen Fitzgibbons, thank you for the recommendations and your love of books.

Rebecca Gradinger: This manuscript has come a long way since our discussions about pony play as a character's "big secret." Thank you for following me down every path and waiting patiently until I found my way to the right book.

Masie Cochran: Your editorial dowsing powers helped me to locate buried words and memories. Without you, this book would have remained a Microsoft Word doc in my computer. I needed you for this.

To my family: I was born into a small family and came of age with a big one. From hogs of both the domesticated and mechanical variety to Thanksgiving oven fires, you've gifted me with writing material and inspiration for the rest of my life. Thank you for your support, your love, your understanding and your attempts at understanding, and for giving me an incomparable childhood.

Kristin: I was a lucky child to have you as a best friend and I am a lucky adult to have the opportunity to express how much our friendship shaped me. Thank you, Kristin, for letting me back into your life.

Antje and Sebastian: You are the best non-blood related family that a girl could have. (And that girl's husband. And that girl's daughter.) Thank you for always being there in every way it's possible to show up.

Domo: To not only have your support for this project, but your love and your encouragement, makes me proud of you, of me, of us. Thank you for being the duck that I'd still choose. Taureau émotion!

Boustic: No, I love you more.

ADDITIONAL RESOURCES

If you don't break your ropes while you're alive
do you think
ghosts will do it after?

—KABIR, *"Hope for the Guest While You Are Alive"*

Should you feel called to either start or return to horseback riding, the United States Equestrian Federation is the national body for equestrian sport. Their website, www.usef.org, has a helpful riding facility locator map, equestrian summer camp listings, information on interscholastic riding programs, and much more. The United States Pony Clubs (www.ponyclub.org) has been teaching riding and proper horse care since 1954, and offers a robust list of programs for youth and adult riders. For polo enthusiasts, the United States Polo Association has a polo club locator tool under the "Learn to Play" tab on their website, www.uspolo.org. The Women's International Polo Network (www.wipnpolo.com) is another excellent place to gather information and resources about this growing sport.

263

The American Hippotherapy Association has an extensive list of practitioners who use equine therapy in their practice via www.americanhippotherapyassociation.org. For traditional talk therapy, *Psychology Today*'s "Find a Therapist" search engine will help you locate quality therapists in your area. If you are having an emotional and/or mental crisis, in Connecticut the crisis hotline is 411; nationally, you can reach help quickly through 1-800-273-TALK.

FURTHER READING

DiMarco, Louis A. *War Horse: A History of the Military Horse and Rider.* Yardley, PA: Westholme Publishing, 2008.

Dreisbach, Verna, ed. *Why We Ride: Women Writers on the Horses in Their Lives.* Berkeley, CA: Seal Press, 2010.

Forrest, Susanna. *The Age of the Horse: An Equine Journey through Human History.* London: Atlantic Books, 2016.

Gonzaga, Paulo Gavião. *A History of the Horse, Volume I: The Iberian Horse from Ice Age to Antiquity.* London: J. A. Allen, 2004.

Marcus, Halimah, ed. *Horse Girls: Recovering, Aspiring, and Devoted Riders Redefine the Iconic Bond.* New York: Harper Perennial, 2021.

Meagher, Colleen McInerney. *Comin' Thru: The Golden Age of Women's Polo 1934–1941.* Mt. Pub Company Inc., 2016.

Pickeral, Tamsin. *The Horse: 30,000 Years of the Horse in Art.* London: Merrell, 2006.

Rosser, Kareem. *Crossing the Line: A Fearless Team of Brothers and the Sport That Changed Their Lives Forever.* New York: St. Martin's Press, 2021.

Selfe, Lorna. *Nadia: A Case of Extraordinary Drawing Ability in an Autistic Child.* New York: A Harvest/HBJ Book, 1977.

Shaffer, Peter. *Equus.* New York: Scribner, 1973.

Swift, Sally. *Centered Riding.* New York: St. Martin's Press, 1985.

Williams, Wendy. *The Horse: The Epic History of Our Noble Companion.* New York: Scientific American / Farrar, Straus and Giroux, 2015.